MARITIME FLAVOURS

Canadian Cataloguing in Publication Data

Lee, Virginia, 1947-
    Maritime flavours
    Includes index.

ISBN 0-88780-252-4

1. Cookery, Canadian — Maritime Provinces
2. Restaurants — Maritime Provinces — Guidebooks.
3. Hotels — Maritime Provinces — Guidebooks.
I. Elliot, Elaine, 1939- II. Title

TX715.6.L43 1994   641.5'09715   C94-950086-0

Formac Publishing Company Limited
5502 Atlantic Street
Halifax Nova Scotia B3H 1G4

Distributed in the U.S. by
Formac Distributing Limited
121 Mount Vernon Street
Boston MA 02108

Printed in Hong Kong

MARITIME FLAVOURS

Guidebook & Cookbook

ELAINE ELLIOT AND VIRGINIA LEE

PHOTOGRAPHY BY KEITH VAUGHAN

Formac Publishing Company Limited

Halifax and Boston

CONTENTS

PREFACE

It is hard to believe that ten years have passed since we acted upon the germ of an idea to combine two of our favourite pastimes — cooking at home for family and friends and dining out. In our first publishing endeavour, *Nova Scotia Inns and Restaurants Cookbook*, published in 1985, we featured recipes from quality restaurants in our home province. The success of this book led us to expand our horizons in 1990 with a second cookbook, *Maritime Inns and Restaurants Cookbook*.

Our third book, *Maritime Flavours*, is an even more ambitious undertaking. With colour photographs as well as recipes, we hope you will find this an especially attractive book and that you will try many of the recipes, savouring these culinary specialities of the Maritime provinces.

We are proud to be Canadians and especially proud to be Maritimers. Our area of the world is rich in beauty, hospitality, heritage and the bounties of nature. *Maritime Flavours* is both a guide book to the many fine inns and restaurants in the region and a source of some favourite creations of our region's best chefs, with an emphasis on the foods that are locally available.

Preparing this book was exciting, fun and, at times, frustrating. We greatly enjoyed visiting the restaurants and inns, sampling fare and deciding which establishments we would invite on board our venture. Testing, tasting and sharing the results with family and friends was exciting. The hard part was deciphering the recipes and converting them to the published format, with quantities appropriate for home cooking.

Maritime Flavours is an independent cookbook and guide, with no sponsorship or fees paid for inclusion. All participating establishments were chosen by us as representing the finest establishments in the three Maritime provinces. Once the selection was made, we approached them to request the recipes we wanted for this book. Almost all were willing and able to share their best recipes with us — and with you.

We offer this book as a celebration of the beauty of our provinces and the quality of our cuisine.

This book is dedicated to our children: Gordon, Stephen and Robert Elliot and Kate, David and Elizabeth Lee.

— *E.E. and V.L.*

LOCATOR MAP

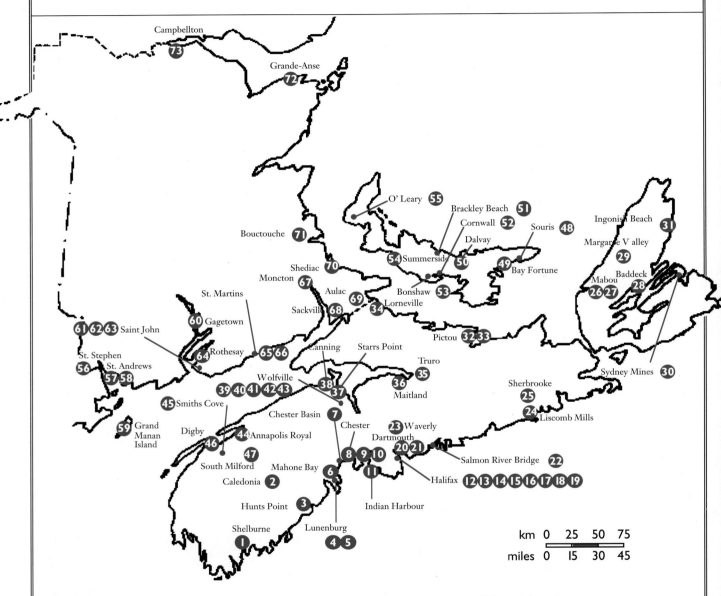

Campbellton 73
Grande-Anse 72

O' Leary 55
Brackley Beach 51
Cornwall 52
Souris 48
Ingonish Beach 31
Bouctouche 71
Dalvay
Margaree Valley
Shediac 70
Summerside 54
Bay Fortune
Mabou 26 27
Baddeck 29
Moncton 67
Aulac 69
Bonshaw 53
28
St. Martins
Sackville 68
Lorneville 34
Gagetown 60
Canning
Starrs Point
Pictou 32 33
Saint John 61 62 63
Rothesay 65 66
Truro 35
Sydney Mines 30
St. Stephen
St. Andrews 64
Wolfville 38 37
Maitland 36
Sherbrooke 25
56
Rossmount 57 58
39 40 41 42 43
The Bright House
Liscomb Mills 24
Smiths Cove 45
Chester Basin 7
Waverly 23
Grand Manan Island 59
Digby 44 Annapolis Royal
Chester
Dartmouth
Salmon River Bridge 22
46
South Milford 47
Mahone Bay
8 9 10
20 21
Caledonia 2
6 11
Halifax 12 13 14 15 16 17 18 19
Indian Harbour
Hunts Point 3
Shelburne 1
Lunenburg 4 5

km 0 25 50 75
miles 0 15 30 45

New Brunswick

The Algonquin, 58
Auberge le Vieux Presbytère de Bouctouche 1880, 71
Aylesford Inn, 73
Chez Françoise, 70
The Compass Rose, 59
Drury Lane Steak House, 69
Dufferin Inn, 63
Gaston's Restaurant, 67
Inn on the Cove, 62

La Poissonnière Restaurant, 72
Loon Bay Lodge, 56
Marshlands Inn, 68
Parkerhouse Inn, 61
Quaco Inn, 65
The Rossmount Inn, 57
Shadow Lawn Country Inn, 64
St. Martins Country Inn, 66
Steamers Stop Inn, 60

Nova Scotia

Acton's Grill and Café, 39
Amherst Shore Country Inn, 34
Bellhill Tea Room, 38
The Blomidon Inn, 40
Bluenose Lodge, 5
The Braeside Inn, 32
The Bright House, 25
Café Chianti, 12
Campbell House, 7
Candleriggs, 11

Tattingstone Inn

APPETIZERS

Classic French cookbooks rarely devote much space to appetizers because it is felt a good cook has the experience and imagination to create his or her own. We feel this may be just a little presumptuous; not everyone has sufficient knowledge of sauces, pastries and the like to be confident to mix, match and create a ravishing gastronomic first course.

We have selected a variety of appetizers from the fine chefs of our Maritime restaurants. Some are extremely simple to prepare while others require a little more time and care. All are delicious and well worth the effort.

Appetizers should appeal to your senses. When guests walk through your door they should be welcomed with a wonderful aroma, something that entices the taste buds. The hearty garlic tomato of *Eggplant Parmigiana* and *Bruschette* from Café Chianti or the delicate herbal aroma of *Mussels Provençale on Toast* from the Walker Inn will heighten their expectations. Other appetizers such as *Seafood Cocktail* from the Rossmount Inn and *Chicken Satay with Peanut Sauce* from Tattingstone Inn have wonderful eye-appeal.

We have included appetizers that are quick and easy, like *Vegetable Crudités* from the Manor Inn, and *Lobster Stuffed Mushroom Caps* from McCrady's Acres, as well as more challenging fare like *Danish Blue Cheesecake in a Walnut Crust with Port Wine Pear Coulis and Spicy Pear Mint Chutney* from the Inn at Bay Fortune.

By increasing the portions of some appetizers, such as *Charbroiled Digby Scallops with Citrus Vinaigrette* from Keltic Lodge, you can easily have a light main course or luncheon dish. Conversely, certain recipes in this cookbook, particularly in the meat, seafood and vegetable sections, when served in smaller portions, make excellent appetizers.

We hope that you will enjoy trying these recipes and perhaps gain a little of that "French confidence" to experiment.

Chicken Satay with Peanut Sauce (Tattingstone Inn)

CHICKEN SATAY WITH PEANUT SAUCE
Tattingstone Inn

At Tattingstone Inn, this wonderful satay with its subtle peanut flavour is served as an appetizer. However, it would make an excellent luncheon dish accompanied by tossed salad and fresh rolls.

1 small red pepper
1 small green pepper
1 small onion
1 pound boneless chicken breast, cut in
    3/4-inch cubes
4 mushrooms
orange and lemon slices
1 tablespoon butter
1 tablespoon flour
pinch of salt
1/2 cup warm milk
1/2 cup peanut butter
3 tablespoons white wine
shredded lettuce

Cut peppers into 3/4 inch square chunks, and onion in quarters. Thread chicken pieces and vegetables on four wooden skewers, until all the chicken is used up. Bake the satays at 375°F, 15 to 20 minutes or until chicken is no longer pink in the center.

While chicken is cooking, prepare white sauce. Melt butter in saucepan over low heat, and blend in flour and salt. Add warm milk all at once. Heat quickly, stirring constantly, until mixture thickens and bubbles. Remove from heat.

Combine peanut butter and white wine with white sauce, and keep warm. If sauce appears too thick, add a little more milk.

To serve, shred lettuce on four appetizer plates. Place satay on lettuce, garnish with thin lemon and orange slices; drizzle with peanut sauce. Serves 4.

EGGPLANT PARMIGIANA
Café Chianti

One would like to duplicate the aromas that waft from the kitchen at Cafe Chianti. By preparing their version of Eggplant Parmigiana it is possible to create those wonderful hearty garlic, tomato and herb fragrances at home.

1 large garlic clove, crushed
1 1/2 teaspoon fresh basil (1 teaspoon dried)
1 1/2 teaspoon fresh oregano (1 teaspoon dried)
dash of salt and pepper
1 medium eggplant, cut in 1/2-inch slices
1 1/2 cups **tomato sauce** (see below)
1 1/2 cups Parmesan cheese (freshly grated)
black olives, red pepper and green onion, for garnish
olive oil

Combine garlic and seasonings and rub into eggplant slices. Arrange eggplant in bottom of 9 x 12-inch shallow casserole dish, overlapping edges if necessary. Spoon tomato sauce over eggplant and sprinkle Parmesan cheese. Bake at 425°F for 10 to 15 minutes until the eggplant is soft and the sauce bubbly.
    Serve on individual dishes. Garnish with black olives, sliced red pepper and julienne green onions which have been tossed in olive oil. Serves 6.

Tomato Sauce
This versatile tomato sauce is a wonderful alternative to the store–bought canned version. It can be used in any recipe calling for a basic tomato sauce. If prepared in larger quantities, it can be frozen for future use.

1/4 cup olive oil
3/4 cup Spanish onion, finely chopped
1 can Italian plum tomatoes (28 ounces)
1/4 teaspoon salt
4-5 turns of pepper grinder

Sauté onion in oil until transparent. Add tomatoes and seasoning and simmer on low heat for 1 hour. Near the end of the cooking time, whisk to break up the tomato. If sauce is too liquid, thicken with a paste of flour and cold water; if too thick, add water. Makes 2 1/2 cups.

VEGETABLE CRUDITÉS
The Manor Inn

An assortment of crisp, fresh vegetables makes this an easy eye-appealing appetizer. In testing we substituted light sour cream and mayonnaise with excellent results.

1 cup sour cream
2 tablespoons mayonnaise
1 tablespoon fresh dill, chopped
1 teaspoon parsley, chopped
1/8 teaspoon lemon juice

Fresh crisp vegetables in bite–size pieces (e.g. carrots, celery, zucchini, broccoli, cauliflower, mushrooms).
    Combine dip ingredients and place in a dish in the center of a platter. Arrange an assortment of vegetables in an attractive fashion around dip. Serves 4 to 6.

BRUSCHETTE
Café Chianti

In the Tuscany area of Italy, dinner begins with a classic "Bruschetta"; a slice of toasted bread spread with garlic and covered with olive oil, tomato slices and basil leaves. Café Chianti's version makes a delicious appetizer or accompaniment to a main course.

1 1/4 cups Spanish onion, finely chopped
2 large, ripe tomatoes, chopped
1/2 cup olive oil
1 tablespoon fresh basil, chopped (1 teaspoon dried)
1 teaspoon fresh oregano, chopped (1/2 teaspoon dried)
1 garlic clove, minced
1 loaf of Italian bread, cut in half, lengthwise
Italian cheese, grated or crumbled

Combine onion, tomatoes, oil, basil, oregano and garlic and mix well. Spread mixture evenly over sliced sides of bread. Top with an Italian cheese such as Boccinni, unripened mozzarella, Romano, Asaigo or Parmesan.
    Bake uncovered on a cookie sheet in preheated 425°F oven for 5 to 6 minutes or until browned and bubbly. Slice to serve.

STEAK TARTARE
The Rossmount Inn

Chefs at the Rossmount Inn find that a fine beef tenderloin, minced and seasoned in the traditional manner, satisfies the most discerning palate.

8 ounces beef tenderloin, cubed
1 tablespoon onion
5 drops Tabasco sauce
7 drops Worcestershire sauce
1/2 egg yolk
5 capers
1 anchovy fillet
salt and pepper
1 teaspoon brandy
chopped fresh parsley
rye bread

Chop the beef very finely, or carefully pulse in a food processor until it is finely ground; remove to a bowl. Process onion, sauces, yolk, capers and anchovy until finely chopped and add to meat. Combine the ingredients in the bowl until they are well blended. Season with salt and pepper to taste. Shape the tartare into a patty and place on a serving dish. Pour brandy over top, garnish with parsley and serve with thin slices rye bread. Serves 4.

SEAFOOD COCKTAIL
The Rossmount Inn

Rossmount Inn steps away from the traditional seafood cocktail served with a tomato–based sauce and instead, offers guests an interesting variation with scallops, shrimp and mussels served in a Dijon-styled vinaigrette. The results is elegant, delicious and easy to prepare.

1 cup water
1/4 cup dry white wine
1 bay leaf
5 black peppercorns
1/4 small onion
1 celery stalk, quartered
24 mussels
12 scallops, halve if large
12 shrimp, peeled and deveined
vinaigrette
6 tomato slices
6 cucumber slices
shredded lettuce
6 lemon wedges
fresh parsley, chopped

In a large pot combine first 6 ingredients, and bring to a boil. Poach mussels for 2 minutes and then add scallops and shrimp and poach for an additional 4 minutes, or until the mussels open and the scallops are just cooked.

Remove seafood from poaching liquid and cool. Remove only 12 of the mussels from their shells and combine *all* the seafood in the vinaigrette. Refrigerate for at least 3 hours.

To serve, divide lettuce among six serving dishes. Top with tomato, cucumber and seafood which has been removed from marinade with a slotted spoon. Garnish with lemon and parsley. Serves 6.

Vinaigrette
1/4 cup olive oil
1/4 cup vegetable oil
1/4 cup red wine vinegar
1 1/2 teaspooons Dijon mustard
1 small garlic clove, crushed
1 tablespoon finely chopped onion
pinch of salt and pepper
pinch of paprika

Combine all ingredients and whisk, or process in a blender, until emulsified.

Kitchen at historic King's Landing

MUSSELS PROVENÇALE ON TOAST
The Walker Inn

You may want to double this recipe because your guests will always want more. It may be the unique way the mussels are used or it could be the wonderful flavour of the delicate Herbes de Provence. Whatever the secret, this appetizer is a winner.

50 mussels
1/4 cup white wine
1 bay leaf
1 tablespoon olive oil
1 large onion, diced
up to 8 small cloves garlic, minced
1 teaspoon flour
salt and pepper to taste
1 tablespoon fresh chopped parsley (1/2 teaspoon dried)
1/2 teaspoon Herbes de Provence *
3/4 cup white wine
1/2 cup heavy cream (35% m.f.)

1 tomato, sliced and heated
4 slices of bread, toasted

Scrub and debeard the mussels, being careful to discard any that are open or have broken shells. In a large pot bring to a boil 1/4 cup of wine with bay leaf and 1 clove of garlic, minced. Add mussels and steam, covered, for 5 minutes or until they open. Discard any that do not fully open when cooked. Remove mussels from shells and reserve.

In a skillet heat olive oil and sauté onion and garlic until softened. Stir the flour into the onion mixture and add the mussels and all seasonings. Gently pour in the remaining 3/4 cup of wine and simmer for 8 to 10 minutes. Stir in the cream and heat slowly, until slightly thickened. Spoon over toast and garnish with hot tomato slices. Serves 4.

* *Herbes de Provence is a delightful combination of dried thyme, rosemary, basil, savory and crushed bay leaf.*

Keltic Lodge

CHARBROILED DIGBY SCALLOPS WITH CITRUS VINAIGRETTE
Keltic Lodge

Colourful, quick and tasty, these appetizers can be prepared in advance and grilled by the host at serving time. Wooden skewers will burn and should be soaked in water for thirty minutes before assembling the kebabs.

1 teaspoon soya sauce
1/4 cup olive oil
1 teaspoon balsamic or sherry vinegar
1 teaspoon lemon juice
2 teaspoons each grapefruit and orange juice
2 teaspoons each lemon, orange, and
    grapefruit zest
1 teaspoon dry pink peppercorns, crushed
salt to taste
3/4 to 1 pound fresh scallops
1/2 each red, yellow and green peppers, cut in
6 squares the size of scallops

6 mushrooms
1 lemon, cut in 6 wedges
assorted salad greens to serve 6
chopped chives

Whisk together first 8 ingredients for the vinaigrette and reserve.

Assemble kebabs, threading scallops, peppers, mushrooms and lemon wedges on skewers. Brush with vinaigrette and grill approximately 3 to 4 minutes per side.

While seafood is cooking, warm remaining vinaigrette. Arrange lettuce leaves on individual salad plates. When ready, place skewers on lettuce and drizzle with remaining vinaigrette. Serves 6.

SPINACH STRUDEL
Nemo's Restaurant

Literally translated, strudel *means "whirlwind". These famous Viennese pastries are made from wafer–thin pastry rolled around a savory or sweet filling. They derive from the Turkish baklava. Nemo's Restaurant creates a savory cheese strudel that is crisp yet melts in your mouth.*

3 cups packed spinach leaves
2/3 cup cream cheese
1/3 cup feta cheese
3 sheets filo pastry
1/4 cup butter, melted

Blanch spinach in boiling water until wilted. Drain well, squeeze out excess water and chop. In a bowl, blend together cheeses and spinach.

Lay 1 filo sheet flat, and spread 1/3 of cheese mixture along the bottom of the pastry. Roll pastry tightly, jelly roll fashion, being careful not to tear. Tuck in ends on last roll. Brush pastry with melted butter and place on a cookie sheet. Repeat procedure.

Bake in a preheated 400°F oven for 7 to 8 minutes until strudels are golden. Remove from heat, cool slightly and cut in 1 1/2-inch segments. Serves 4 as an appetizer or 2 dozen as hors d'oeuvre. This recipe was tested with "light" cream cheese.

LOBSTER STUFFED MUSHROOM CAPS
McCrady's Green Acres

Chef David Bradshaw combines garlic butter and fresh lobster to create these delightful hot mushroom treats.

1/4 cup butter
2 garlic cloves, crushed
20 small mushroom caps, stems removed
3 tablespoons diced onion
1 cup cooked lobster
mozzarella cheese, grated

Combine butter and crushed garlic cloves to make garlic butter. In a skillet, sauté mushroom caps and onion in garlic butter until mushrooms are softened. Remove mushroom caps to

escargot dishes. Add lobster to skillet and heat through. Place a piece of lobster in each mushroom. Cover mushrooms with any residue from skillet and top with grated mozzarella cheese. Broil in a preheated oven until the cheese is golden and bubbly. Serves 4.

SAUTÉED MUSHROOMS
The Braeside Inn

The delicate mushroom flavour is given a zip with the Tabasco in this appetizer from Pictou's Braeside Inn.

3/4 pound mushrooms,
3 to 4 tablespoons vegetable oil
1 garlic clove, minced
2 shakes of Tabasco sauce
3/4 teaspoon oregano
salt and pepper to taste
1 1/2 teaspoons lemon juice
1 1/2 tablespoons white wine
red pepper, for garnish

Quarter or halve larger mushrooms so that all pieces are a uniform size. Preheat skillet on high heat. Add oil and mushrooms and sauté for 30 seconds. Season with garlic, Tabasco, oregano, salt and pepper and continue to sauté until mushrooms are lightly browned. Add lemon juice and wine. Bring to a boil and immediately remove from heat. Serve mushrooms in small heated casserole dishes garnished with a fan of slivered red pepper. Serves 4 to 6.

Braeside Inn

Quaco Inn

DANISH BLUE CHEESECAKE IN A WALNUT CRUST WITH PORT WINE PEAR COULIS AND SPICY PEAR MINT CHUTNEY
The Inn at Bay Fortune

Chef Michael Smith's careful blending of fruits, nuts and cheeses makes this dish an extraordinary visual and flavourful treat.

12 ounces walnuts
3 large plain shredded wheat
2 tablespoons butter
8 ounces cream cheese
8 ounces blue cheese
4 eggs

Grind walnuts in a food processor. Add shredded wheat and butter and combine just until wheat breaks up. Press crust mix into an 8 inch springform pan and set in a 300°F oven for 5 minutes. Remove from oven and cool.
   Cream together the cheeses until thoroughly combined. Add eggs and mix well. Pour into prepared crust and bake at 350°F until set, approximately 60 minutes. Chill.

Port Wine Pear Coulis
2 ripe pears
1/2 cup port

Remove core and seeds. Rough chop pears and simmer in port 20 minutes. Cool and purée.

Pear Mint Chutney
1 medium onion, finely diced
1/2 jalapeño pepper, chopped (or to taste)
1/4 cup cider vinegar
1/2 teaspoon ground cloves
2 ripe pears, diced
1/2 cup fresh mint leaves (tied in cheesecloth)

Simmer onion and chopped jalapeño in vinegar until soft. Add cloves and pear, simmer 5 additional minutes. Add mint and refrigerate overnight. At serving time remove mint leaves.
   To serve, warm cheesecake and serve a small wedge on the pear coulis with a dollop of chutney on top. Yields 8 to 10 servings.

STUFFED MUSSELS APPETIZER
Gaston's Restaurant

Mussels are a Maritime speciality and this hors d'oeuvre can be prepared in advance, frozen, and kept on hand for a special dinner or unexpected guests.

1 cup bechamel or medium white sauce (see page 48)
32 medium mussels, scrubbed and debearded
1/2 cup cooked lobster meat, chopped
6 medium scallops, cooked and chopped
6 jumbo shrimp, cooked and chopped
salt and pepper, to taste
2 eggs
1 cup milk
1 cup flour
1 cup dry breadcrumbs
6 tablespoons Parmesan cheese

Prepare white sauce and chill.
Steam mussels in small amount of water until cooked and shells open. Cool under running water discarding any that do not open. Remove and discard one half of each shell.
Add lobster, scallops and shrimps to the white sauce and season with salt and pepper. Put a spoonful of seafood mixture on the top of each mussel in its half shell. Place mussels on a baking sheet and freeze.
Combine egg and milk. Coat frozen mussels with flour, dip in egg wash and then in bread crumbs. Arrange mussels on a baking sheet and top with cheese. Bake at 350°F for 20 minutes or until slightly browned and bubbly. Serves 4-6.

TERIYAKI WRAP UPS
The Whitman Inn

Nancy Gurnham loves to experiment and create new food sensations. She serves these hot little appetizers along with a variety of other innovative hors d'oeuvres for special occasions.

1 tablespoon brown sugar
1 tablespoon honey
2 tablespoons soy sauce
1/4 cup water

1/4 cup sake (optional dry sherry)
1–inch piece fresh ginger, peeled and grated
3 cloves garlic, crushed
1/4 teaspoon dashi powder*
2 green onions, finely chopped
1/2 lb flank steak, cut in thin strips on the diagonal
1/2 lb scallops
1 can water chestnuts, drained

Make marinade by whisking together first nine ingredients.
Place steak, scallops and water chestnuts in a bowl. Pour marinade over, and stir. Let stand 1 hour.
Wrap each steak strip around 1 scallop and 1 water chestnut and secure with a toothpick. Arrange wrap-ups on a baking sheet and bake in a preheated 350°F oven for 20 to 25 minutes or until the meat is cooked. Serve as an hors d'oeuvre.

*Sold in Oriental specialty shops.

STUFFED MUSHROOM APPETIZERS
Quaco Inn

Marilyn Landry often serves guests an appetizer tray in the living room before dinner. She tells us that the stuffed mushrooms are always the first to disappear!

20 - 24 large mushrooms
1/2 cup mayonnaise
1/2 cup sour cream
garlic powder or onion powder to taste
1/2 - 11 oz. can frozen lobster, drained
paprika, for garnish

Clean mushrooms and remove stems. Chop stems, add mayonnaise, sour cream, garlic or onion powder and chopped lobster. Spoon into mushroom crowns and garnish with a dash of paprika. Serve chilled.

Gazpacho (The Captain's House)

SOUPS

There is nothing more satisfying than a bowl of homemade soup and Maritime chefs have developed a number of regional specialities that will fulfill the expectations of the most discerning palates.

Soups are economical and easy to prepare. They can be served as an appetizer course or when accompanied by a salad, make an excellent luncheon choice. The thick seafood chowders which have made Maritime cooks famous are hearty enough to be served as an entrée.

When collecting these recipes we asked cooks to share their regional favourites and we were pleasantly surprised by their variety and ingenuity. Sophisticated chilled offerings, such as Gowrie House's *Chilled Melon Soup* or the *Gazpacho* served at the Captain's House of Chester, are a refreshingly different way to begin a summer meal. Keltic's *Chilled Peach Soup* adapts well to a variety of garnishes and is a delightful combination of fruity flavours.

New Brunswick produces an abundant fiddlehead crop and recipes for their use abound. *Cream of Fiddlehead Soup* from the Aylesford Inn in Campbellton best portrays the subtle flavour of this delicate fern. Summer vegetables blend nicely in creamed soups and *Asparagus Soup with Cream and Parmesan* from Cooper's Inn or *Cream of Greens Soup* from the Bright House cannot be surpassed as warm soups with delicate flavours.

Be sure to try one of our famous Maritime chowders! While every cook has a favourite chowder recipe, we suggest you try the simple *Mussel Chowder with Thyme* as prepared by the Shadow Lawn Country Inn of Rothesay, or *Seafood Chowder* from the Palliser Restaurant. The *Mussel Chowder* is characterized by its herbs, while the *Seafood Chowder* is a feast of whitefish and shellfish. The chefs suggest that as a chowder's flavour is enhanced by refrigerating overnight, these are ideal dishes to prepare a day ahead.

Gowrie House

CHILLED MELON SOUP WITH MINT
Gowrie House Country Inn

The sweet flavour of melons combined with the tang of orange and lime makes Chilled Melon Soup with Mint a hit with summertime guests. It is refreshing, delicious and easy to prepare.

1 cantaloup, peeled, seeded and cubed
1/4 Cranshaw, Santa Claus or Cassaba melon, peeled, seeded and cubed
1/2 honeydew melon, peeled, seeded and cubed
1/2 mango, peeled and cubed
1 cup fresh orange juice
3 tablespoons fresh lime juice
2 tablespoons honey
1/3 cup fresh mint leaves, coarsely chopped
1 cup seeded watermelon cut in 1/2-inch cubes
1 cup sparkling white wine
sour cream and mint leaves, as garnish

In a food processor, purée, melons (except watermelon), mango, honey, mint, orange and lime juice. Pour into a non-metal container; stir in wine and watermelon and chill for several hours or overnight. Serve cold with a dollop of sour cream and a sprig of mint. Serves 6.

BLUE MUSSEL AND SWEET POTATO CHOWDER WITH SPICY BUTTER
The Inn At Bay Fortune

The Inn at Bay Fortune's rendition of mussel chowder is far from ordinary. In fact, chef Michael Smith's creation has fresh Island mussels surrounded in a golden coloured sweet potato soup and topped with a very spicy butter. Very different — very good!

3 pounds mussels
1 cup water
2 large sweet potatoes, peeled and shredded
1 medium onion, chopped
2 large stalks celery, chopped
2 cups milk
salt and pepper to taste
1/2 cup fresh parsley, chopped

Spicy Butter
2 tablespoons heavy cream, (32% mf)
1/4 cup brown sugar
1/4 teaspoon ground cloves
1/4 teaspoon cayenne pepper
1/4 cup butter

Prepare mussels by debearding and discarding any that do not close when rinsed under cold water. In a large pot, bring water to a boil, add mussels and steam until mussels open (approximately 6 minutes). Discard any mussels that do not open. Strain mussel liquid and reserve. Remove mussels from shells and refrigerate.

Simmer sweet potatoes, onion and celery in milk and mussel liquid for 30 minutes. (The milk will separate when cooking but will cream again when puréed.) Cool and purée in batches. This chowder is best when made one day in advance and reheated just prior to serving.

Prepare **Spicy Butter** by bringing cream, brown sugar and spices to a simmer in a small saucepan. Slowly, whisk in butter until combined.

To serve, add the mussels and parsley to the chowder and gently reheat. Serve in individual bowls topped with a drizzling of hot Spicy Butter. Serves 4 to 6.

KELTIC'S CHILLED PEACH SOUP
Keltic Lodge

Everything about Keltic Lodge is spectacular. The hospitality, the scenery and this chilled version of soup. If fresh strawberries are not in season, garnish with kiwi slices or other fruits.

8 fresh peaches (or 19 ounces canned peaches
    drained)
1/4 cup fine white sugar
1 cup sweet white wine
2 cups water
pinch of cinnamon
1 cup white wine (2nd amount)
8 large strawberries, sliced for garnish

Make a cross on the top of each peach and drop into boiling water for 30 seconds and then in

Keltic Lodge

cool water until the skin comes off. Remove the pits and chop.

In a medium pot combine sugar, wine, water, cinnamon and peaches. Simmer on low until peaches are soft. Pour into a food processor and purée. Press mixture through a coarse strainer. Add the 2nd amount of white wine and chill overnight. Serve with sliced strawberries as a garnish. Yields 6 to 8 servings.

Zuppa Di Pesce al Modenese (La Perla)

ZUPPA DI PESCE AL MODENESE
La Perla

Six years ago enthusiastic customers persuaded Pearl MacDougall to expand her small café. Today, this cream and tomato seafood soup, featuring fresh scallops, shrimp and mussels, is an example of the fine fare found on the extensive menu at La Perla.

5 cups fish stock*
1/4 teaspoon saffron
1/4 teaspoon fennel seeds
2 tablespoons olive oil
2 garlic cloves, crushed
2 stalks celery, finely chopped
1 leek, chopped
1/2 cup white wine
4 tomatoes, peeled and chopped
1 tablespoon fresh tarragon, chopped
    (1 teaspoon dried)
1 tablespoon fresh parsley, chopped
    (1 teaspoon dried)
1 teaspoon dried oregano
1/2 cup tomato sauce

1 pound mussels, scrubbed and debearded
1 pound white fish (cod, haddock etc.)
1/2 pound shrimp, shelled and deveined
1/4 pound scallops
4 squid, tubes cut into rings
1 carrot, cut in thin slivers with carrot peeler
2 basil leaves, chopped or a pinch of dried

Bring stock to boil and add saffron and fennel seeds. Meanwhile heat oil in a skillet and sauté garlic, celery and leeks until softened. Deglaze skillet with wine and add tomatoes and herbs. Cook for a few minutes and then add mixture to stock along with tomato sauce. Simmer 20 minutes.

Add mussels to soup and 2 minutes later add the remaining seafood and carrot slivers. Simmer for 5 minutes. Serve immediately topped with a pinch of fresh basil leaves. Serves 6.

*Powdered fish stock available in most supermarkets may be substituted for pure fish stock. Follow directions on package.

GAZPACHO
The Captain's House

Though a Spanish soup, the name gazpacho is Arabic in origin and means "soaked bread". The combination of puréed vegetables, olive oil, bread and herbs served ice-cold is a great cooler on a hot summer's day.

3 slices brown or wholewheat bread, cut into
    1-inch cubes
1 1/4 cups tomato juice
2 garlic cloves, minced
1/2 cucumber, peeled and finely chopped
1 medium green pepper, seeded and finely
    chopped
1 medium red pepper, seeded and finely
    chopped
1 medium onion, finely chopped
1 1/2 pounds tomatoes, blanched, peeled,
    seeded and chopped
1/3 cup olive oil
2 tablespoons red wine vinegar
1/2 teaspoon salt
1/4 teaspoon black pepper, freshly ground
1/2 teaspoon fresh marjoram, chopped
1/2 teaspoon fresh basil, chopped
4 ice cubes

Soak bread cubes in tomato juice in a mixing bowl for 5 minutes. Add the garlic, cucumber, peppers, onion and tomatoes to the bread cubes and stir to mix thoroughly. Transfer this mixture to a food processor and purée. Add the oil, vinegar and seasoning to processor and briefly process. The soup should be the consistency of light cream. Add more tomato juice, if necessary.

    Turn soup into a deep serving bowl and place it in the refrigerator to chill for at least 1 hour. Just before serving, stir the soup well and drop in ice cubes. Serves 4.

Shadow Lawn

MUSSEL CHOWDER WITH THYME
Shadow Lawn Country Inn

Chef Frank Gallant added a little thyme to make this simple mussel chowder a gourmet's delight. Try it on a cold winter evening!

3 pounds mussels, scrubbed and debearded
1/4 cup white wine (or water)
4 medium potatoes, peeled and diced
2 onions, diced
1/4 cup butter
1/4 cup flour
4 cups milk
salt, pepper and thyme to taste

Steam prepared mussels in wine until shells open, about 5 minutes. Discard any that do not open. Take meat out of shells and reserve.

    Boil potatoes in liquid from mussels and set aside.

    In a separate saucepan, sauté onions in butter, being careful not to brown them. Add flour and cook 5 minutes, stirring constantly. Slowly whisk in milk and heat until nearly to the boiling point. Add potatoes and their liquid, then add mussels. Season to taste with salt, pepper and thyme. Serves 4 to 6.

Indian Harbour, N.S.

ASPARAGUS SOUP WITH CREAM AND PARMESAN
Cooper's Inn and Restaurant

This is a wonderful soup to prepare in late spring when the local asparagus season is at its height. We also tried this recipe using a combination of light cream (10% bf) and milk and though the result wasn't as creamy, it was lower in fat content and just as yummy!

1 pound fresh asparagus
1 leek
2 garlic cloves, minced
2 tablespoons olive oil
1/4 cup unsalted butter
2 medium potatoes, peeled and cubed
2 1/2 cups chicken stock
1 cup heavy cream (32% mf)
Parmesan cheese, grated
black pepper, freshly ground

Clean and prepare the asparagus by discarding the ends of the stalks. Remove the green top of the leek and rinse white part thoroughly, removing any grit. Slice in 1-inch lengths.

Heat oil and butter in a large saucepan and sauté leeks and garlic. Add potatoes and broth and boil until the potatoes are barely tender. Add the asparagus and cook until just done, being careful not to overcook.

Remove the asparagus with tongs, cut off and reserve the tips. Place the asparagus stock, and other vegetables in a food processor and purée. Strain the purée through a fine sieve or food mill. Add reserved asparagus tips and cream to the soup and reheat, being careful not to boil. Serve in bowls garnished with a generous grating of Parmesan cheese and black pepper. Serves 4.

TOMATO BISQUE
The Innlet Café

This tangy soup is quickly prepared using ingredients commonly found on your pantry shelf.

1 can tomato paste (5.5 ounces)
1 teaspoon brown sugar
1 teaspoon chervil, dried
3 teaspoons celery salt
1/8 teaspoon pepper (4-5 grinds pepper mill)
1 1/4 cups water
3 1/3 cups homogenized milk

In a saucepan whisk together tomato paste, sugar and seasonings. Slowly whisk in water and milk. Heat over medium heat whisking occasionally until it is piping hot. Serve immediately. Serves 4.

THREE ONION SOUP
MacAskill's Restaurant

It is wonderful to be around when French Onion Soup is being prepared. The compulsion to have a taste is almost unbearable. MacAskill's unique version that combines three varieties of onion with a little tomato paste and a pinch of herbs is just as compelling.

2 tablespoons vegetable oil
1/2 bunch green onions, sliced thinly
3/4 pound red onions, sliced thinly
3/4 pound Spanish onions, sliced thinly
pinch of dried oregano
pinch of dried basil
1 cup dry red wine
2 tablespoons tomato paste
8 cups beef stock
croutons or sliced French bread, toasted
mozzarella cheese, grated

In a large stock pot, heat oil and sauté onions until softened, about 4 minutes. Add herbs and red wine and simmer 10 minutes. Add tomato paste and stock, cover and and simmer 45 minutes. Place soup in individual bowls, top with croutons or toasted bread and a generous layer of grated cheese. Place under broiler until cheese is brown and bubbly. Serves 6 to 8.

The Liscomb River at Liscombe Lodge

TOMATO GIN SOUP
Liscombe Lodge

Prepare this classic tomato soup a day in advance and let the flavours blend and mellow. We served it with an assortment of crackers and Brie cheese.

2 tablespoons vegetable oil
1 medium onion, diced
4 strips lean bacon diced
1 clove garlic, crushed
3/4 cup fresh mushrooms, sliced
1 1/2 teaspoon dried sweet basil
1 1/2 teaspoon dried thyme
2 cups chicken stock
3 cups tomato juice
1 pound tomatoes, blanched, peeled and seeds
    removed (or 19-ounce can of whole
    tomatoes)
dash tabasco sauce
dash Worcestershire sauce
1/4 cup gin
salt and pepper

Sauté onion, bacon and garlic in vegetable oil until bacon is cooked but not crisp. Add mushrooms, basil, thyme, stock, juice, tomatoes, tabasco, Worcestershire sauce, and gin. Season with salt and pepper and simmer 45 minutes to 1 hour on low heat. Adjust seasonings if necessary. Yields 6 servings.

SEAFOOD CHOWDER
The Palliser

Never visit the Maritimes without sampling the renowned seafood chowders! The Palliser's creamy version is filled with seafood and simply delicious.

1/4 cup butter
1/4 cup chicken bouillon powder
1/4 teaspoon white pepper
1 cup water
4 cups blend (or milk or combination of both)
2 tablespoons butter (2nd amount)
1 cup diced celery
1 cup diced onion
1 pound haddock, 1-inch cubes
3/4 pound scallops, halve if large
1/2 pound frozen lobster and juice (if using

fresh lobster, retain 3/4 cup of the cooking
    liquid as juice)
1/2 cup flour
2 cups milk

In a large, heavy-bottomed saucepan melt butter and stir in powdered bouillon and pepper. Add water and blend and keep warm over low heat, being careful not to boil.

In a large skillet melt 2nd amount of butter; sauté celery and onion until softened. Add haddock, scallops, lobster and juice and cook until seafood is barely cooked. Transfer seafood to a saucepan.

In a bowl, slowly whisk milk into flour, beating until smooth. Pour this through a strainer into soup and heat soup until thickened and steamy. Again, be careful not to let the soup come to a boil as the milk will separate. Serves 6 to 8 generously.

COBEQUID BAY STEW
Cobequid Inn

Innkeepers Nancy and Jim Cleveland gave this unique name to their hearty tomato–based soup because it is red like the tidal waters of Cobequid Bay that flow near the inn.

2 pounds lean ground beef
6 cups tomato juice
1 cup stewed tomatoes with juice
1 cup sliced mushrooms (or 1 can, drained)
2 cups thinly sliced celery
2 cups thinly sliced carrots
2 cups chopped cabbage
2 onions, diced
1 teaspoon basil
1 teaspoon garlic powder
1 teaspoon Worcestershire sauce
1 bay leaf
2 teaspoons dried oregano
salt and pepper to taste

In a skillet brown the beef and then drain well to remove all excess fat. In a large soup pot combine all ingredients and stir well. Bring to a boil and then reduce heat to low and simmer for 1 to 1 1/2 hours. Adjust seasoning to taste. This soup is excellent for the cold days of fall and winter. Yields 10 large servings.

TOMATO-ZUCCHINI SOUP
Auberge le Vieux Presbytère de Bouctouche 1880

This is a wonderful summer soup! Make it when you have an abundant crop of zucchini and fresh basil is at its peak.

1/4 cup vegetable oil
1 medium onion, chopped
1 pound zucchini, chopped into 1/2-inch dice
4 cups tomato juice
1 3/4 cups chicken broth
2 1/2 teaspoons Worcestershire sauce
3/4 teaspoon salt
3/4 teaspoon sugar
dash of cayenne
1 teaspoon dried basil
fresh basil to garnish

Heat oil in a stockpot over moderate heat. Add onion and zucchini and cook until onion is soft, about 5 minutes. Add tomato juice, broth, Worcestershire sauce, salt, sugar, cayenne and basil. Bring to a boil, then reduce heat and simmer, covered, for 5 to 8 minutes to blend flavours. Garnish each serving with a sprig of fresh basil. Serves 6.

CREAM OF GREENS SOUP
The Bright House

Sometimes the simple things in life are the most treasured. This tasty soup is easy to prepare. Its colour depends on the green vegetables you choose to include.

Green Vegetable Purée
2 cups water
2 cups chicken stock
2 onions, chopped
1 large carrot, finely chopped
2 stalks celery with leaves, sliced
5 to 6 cups of any combination of chopped
     green vegetables, such as broccoli, green
     onion, zucchini, lettuce, spinach.

Put all ingredients in a large pot and bring to a boil. Simmer until all vegetables are soft. Purée in batches in a food processor and return

to pot. The purée should be the consistency of thick tomato juice and measure 8 cups. Add more stock if too thick and add powdered chicken base in a little hot water if the purée needs more flavour.

Cream Sauce
3 tablespoons butter
3 tablespoons flour
3 cups milk
1 teaspoon curry powder, or to taste
salt and pepper
1 cup sour cream (tested using low-fat)
dill weed

Melt butter in a saucepan and stir in flour forming a roux. Whisk in milk, curry powder, salt and pepper and continue stirring until sauce is bubbly and thickened. Add cream sauce to vegetable purée. Adjust seasoning and return to serving temperature. Stir in 3/4 cup of the sour cream. Serve with a dollop of the remaining sour cream and a sprinkling of dill weed. Serves 6 to 8 generous portions.

Blue mussels

CREAM OF FIDDLEHEAD SOUP
Aylesford Inn

Shirley Ayles picks her fiddleheads and grows her own herbs to prepare this classic New Brunswick soup. While not quite as good as the fresh version, you can find fiddleheads in the frozen food section of most large supermarkets, and should follow the cooking directions on the package.

1 pound fiddleheads, washed and tails trimmed
1 potato, peeled and cubed
2 cups water
3 tablespoons butter
3 tablespoons flour
4 cups milk
1/2 cup heavy cream (35% m.f.)
salt and pepper, to taste
1/4 teaspoon dried tarragon
1/2 teaspoon dried rosemary
2 teaspoons dried chervil
1 teaspoon dried parsley

Cook fiddleheads and potatoes in the water until tender. In the meantime, melt butter in a saucepan and whisk in flour. Slowly whisk in 2 cups of the milk and cook over medium heat until slightly thickened.

Reserve six fiddleheads for garnish, then place potato and fiddleheads in a blender with their cooking liquid and purée. Add sauce mixture, remaining milk, cream and spices. Return to saucepan and reheat being careful not to boil. Garnish each bowl with a whole cooked fiddlehead. Serves 6.

Waterford, N.B.

Bay of Fundy fishing weir

SEAFOOD CHOWDER
The Algonquin

And yet another wonderful Maritime seafood chowder! The Algonquin's version is very substantial — with chunks of lobster, halibut, haddock, scallops, and vegetables in a creamy base.

1 pound seafood (combination of lobster, salmon, halibut, scallops and shrimp)
2 cups water
1 1/2 tablespoon butter
1/4 cup each red and green pepper, diced
1/4 onion, diced
1/2 cup butter (2nd amount)
1/2 cup flour
reserved poaching liquid plus fish stock to make 4 cups
1 cup table cream (18% m.f.)
salt and pepper to taste

Prepare fish in bite-size pieces and poach in water for 5 to 6 minutes. Drain, reserving liquid. Melt 1 1/2 tablespoons of butter in a skillet and sauté peppers and onions until tender but not brown.

Melt butter (2nd amount) in the top of a large double boiler over simmering water. Add flour, blending well. Whisk in stock and reserved poaching liquid and stir constantly until the first bubbles appear and it starts to boil. Reduce the heat and cook 30 minutes stirring frequently.

Transfer vegetables and seafood to a large pot, add sauce, cream and seasoning. Heat, but do not boil. Serves 4.

The Algonquin

Marinated Carrot Salad (The Galley)

SALADS

The early Romans seem to have been the originators of salads but they liked their greens served with just a sprinkling of salt. It is not surprising that the salads we have chosen for this book show more ingenuity. We bet that Julius Caesar would have preferred La Poissonnière's rendition of *Julius Caesar's Shrimp Salad* over his usual fare. In fact it is quite possibly the best Caesar salad we have ever tasted.

Many of the recipes, like *Moroccan Chicken Salad* from Gaston's Restaurant, include seafood and meats and can be served as a light meal. As well, *Potato and Mussel Salad* from the Strathgartney Country Inn, featuring local Island potatoes and cultivated mussels, is an ample luncheon dish.

In an effort to promote healthy eating, we have tested recipes using oils with lower cholesterol, such as olive and canola. Recipes calling for yoghurt, sour cream and mayonnaise we retested using low fat equivalents. We did not notice any appreciable difference in taste. Salads incorporating yoghurt include the *Cucumber Slaw* from the Shadow Lawn Country Inn and chef Don Campbell's *Tomato and Cucumber Salad*. Both are light, crisp and ideal for the health conscious.

We are sure that there will be a favourite salad for everyone in this book!

The Galley

MARINATED CARROT SALAD
The Galley

Maritime cooks have a talent for using what is available to them, especially during the long, cold winter months. This carrot salad is an excellent example and tastes great in the calorie-conscious version, using the lesser amount of sugar.

1 can tomato soup (10-ounces)
1/2 to 1 cup sugar
1/2 cup vegetable oil
3/4 cup cider vinegar
1 teaspoon prepared mustard
1 teaspoon salt
1 teaspoon freshly ground pepper
2 tablespoons fresh dill, chopped or
    2 teaspoons dry
6 cups carrot sticks, blanched but still crunchy
    to bite
1 cup celery sticks
1 cup diced onion

For salad dressing, shake first eight ingredients in a jar and pour over vegetables. Let marinate several hours. Serve on a bed of lettuce and garnish with sprigs of fresh dill. Serves 6 to 8.

HALLIBURTON SALAD WITH MANDARIN POPPY SEED DRESSING
Halliburton House Inn

At the Halliburton House Inn, this tangy salad is served on a plate of crisp salad greens, drizzled with dressing and topped with crunchy almonds.

1/4 cup chopped onion
1 1/2 teaspoons sugar
1 1/2 teaspoons Dijon mustard
1 1/2 teaspoons dry mustard
2 tablespoons cider vinegar
3/4 cup vegetable oil

1 tablespoon poppy seeds
1/2 cup drained mandarin segments
2 cups each spinach, romaine and iceberg
    lettuce
1 large carrot, in julienne strips
2 tomatoes, seeded and pulp removed and
    cut in strips
1 leek, in julienne strips
slivered almonds, toasted

Purée onion and sugar in a food processor, and add mustards and cider vinegar. Continue processing adding oil in a slow stream until emulsified. Stir in poppy seeds and mandarin segments.

Divide greens among 4 chilled salad plates. Arrange vegetables in concentric circles on greens. Drizzle dressing over salad and top with almonds. Serves 4.

CUCUMBER SLAW
Shadow Lawn Country Inn

The Shadow Lawn is an elegant and inviting location for receptions and dinners. Chef Frank Gallant likes to serve this healthy slaw with fresh salmon entrées.

1 large English cucumber
1 1/2 teaspoons salt
1 tablespoon chopped chives
1 teaspoon chopped fresh dill
1/4 cup plain skim-milk yoghurt

Cut cucumber in quarters lengthwise. Remove seeds and grate on a medium grater. Place cucumber in a bowl, sprinkle with salt and stir to mix. Refrigerate 2 hours. Drain and rinse cucumber in a sieve, removing all excess moisture.

In a medium bowl whisk together chives, dill and yoghurt. Stir cucumbers into yoghurt sauce. Serves 4 to 6.

JULIUS CAESAR'S SHRIMP SALAD
La Poissonnière

Richard Chiasson's version of the classic Caesar salad is truly fit for an emperor. If you try only one recipe from this book, let this be the one!

2 egg yolks
1 clove garlic, minced
1 teaspoon Dijon mustard
1 teaspoon capers, chopped fine
6 drops Worcestershire sauce
2 drops hot pepper sauce (Tabasco)
1-inch by 1/2-inch piece smoked herring,
    chopped fine
1 cup vegetable oil
2 tablespoons vinegar
2 tablespoons fresh lemon juice
1/4 cup Parmesan cheese
salt and pepper, to taste
1 head Romaine lettuce
4 ounces fresh baby shrimp
1/2 cup croutons
6 lemon wedges, as garnish

Using a glass bowl and a wire whisk, mix yolks, garlic, mustard, capers, Worcestershire sauce, Tabasco and herring until it forms a paste. Slowly add oil as you continue beating, then add vinegar, lemon, Parmesan cheese, salt and pepper. Chill dressing while you prepare the salad.

Clean and wash romaine lettuce, spin dry. Break lettuce into bite-size pieces and place in a large salad bowl with baby shrimp and croutons. Just before serving add enough dressing to lightly coat lettuce and toss. Serve each portion with a lemon wedge and extra cheese on the side. Serves 6.

TOMATO AND CUCUMBER SALAD
Campbell House

A hint of mint gives this salad a unique flavor. Testing with low-fat yoghurt and light sour cream did not compromise the results!

1/3 English cucumber, seeded and thinly sliced
1 medium tomato, diced
1/2 cup plain yoghurt
1/3 cup sour cream
1 teaspoon concentrated mint sauce
1 tablespoon chopped parsley
pinch each of salt, white pepper and coriander
1 head Romaine lettuce
1 teaspoon chopped parsley for garnish
2 lemon wedges

Prepare cucumber and tomato and place in a bowl. Combine yoghurt, sour cream, mint sauce, chopped parsley, salt, pepper and coriander and mix until well blended. Pour over tomato and cucumber and refrigerate one hour. To serve, chop lettuce and place in bowls. Spoon chilled mixture over Romaine and garnish with parsley and lemon wedges. Four regular or two generous servings.

ALMOND AND BROCCOLI SALAD
Steamers Stop Inn

Bright reds, greens and whites make this salad an eye-appealing delight which the chef tells us improves in flavour if prepared a day in advance.

1 pound broccoli, cut into bite-size pieces
1 medium red onion, chopped
1 tomato, seeds removed chopped
1/2 cup slivered almonds, toasted*
1 small cauliflower, cut in bite-size pieces (optional)

Dressing
1 teaspoon white sugar
1/4 cup vegetable oil
1/4 cup white vinegar
1 tablespoon prepared mustard
1 tablespoon chopped onion

Place vegetables and almonds in a large bowl.
Combine dressing ingredients in a food processor or blender. Pour over vegetables and marinate, stirring several times, 3 to 4 hours. Yields 4 to 6 servings.

* Toast almonds in a shallow pan in a 300°F oven for several minutes. Stir frequently until they are a pale golden colour.

SPINACH MANDARIN SALAD
Loon Bay Lodge

The Loon Bay Lodge version of a mandarin salad with crisp bacon and fresh mushrooms is a bit more substantial than most and makes an attractive luncheon choice.

Salad greens to serve 6 to 8 (spinach, Romaine and iceberg)
2 green onions, chopped
1/2 cup mushrooms, sliced
1/2 can mandarin orange segments, drained, reserving juice
3 slices bacon, cooked crisp and crumbled
1/4 cup slivered almonds, toasted
1/2 cup sugar
1/2 cup vegetable oil
1/2 cup vinegar
1/2 cup reserved mandarin juice
salt and pepper

Wash and spin-dry greens and break into bite-size pieces. Place in a large salad bowl, and add green onions, mushrooms, mandarin segments and crumbled bacon.
Combine sugar, oil, vinegar, mandarin juice, salt and pepper. Shake to blend well and toss with vegetables. Top salad with toasted almond slivers. Serves 6 to 8.

Fortress Louisbourg

PASTA SALAD
Gowrie House Country Inn

Clifford Matthews, co-owner and chef at Gowrie House Country Inn, loves to cook and to please his guests with his food innovations. This colourful and healthy Pasta Salad is an example of Clifford's maxim to use only the freshest and best ingredients available to him.

1 pound fresh rotini pasta
1/3 cup olive oil
1 large or 2 small garlic cloves, crushed
4 cups assorted vegetables, blanched (julienne carrots, sliced zucchini, broccoli and cauliflower flowerets, snow peas, asparagus)
2 cups vegetables, unblanched (green onions, cubed celery and sweet peppers, peas)

Dressing
zest from 1 lemon (thin peel)
juice from 2 lemons (about 6 tablespoons)
1 tablespoon Dijon mustard
1 cup olive oil
freshly ground pepper to taste
salt to taste

Cook pasta in a large pot of boiling salted water, according to directions, until al dente. Drain and refresh pasta under cold water. In a large bowl combine 1/3 cup oil and garlic. Add pasta and stir to coat evenly. Set aside for at least 1 hour.

Prepare vegetables, blanching the crisper ones for one minute and refreshing under cold water to stop cooking process. Reserve vegetables in refrigerator.

Meanwhile, prepare dressing. Combine lemon zest, juice and mustard in a food processor and continue processing while slowly adding oil until dressing is emulsified. Add salt and pepper to taste.

To prepare salad, combine pasta and vegetables, pour dressing over and stir to combine well. Serve pasta at room temperature on lettuce leaves with a scattering of chopped fresh parsley.

This recipe makes a large salad. It may be halved to serve 4 to 6 but author suggests making the full recipe as the leftovers will keep for several days, refrigerated.

Bay of Fundy shore at St. Martins, N.B.

CELERY SEED DRESSING
Drury Lane Steak House

The chef at Drury Lane says, "This dressing is sweet but slightly tart at the same time. The celery seed gives it an unusual zesty flavour."

1 teaspoon dry mustard
1 teaspoon salt
scant 1/2 cup white sugar
1 teaspoon grated onion
1/3 cup + 1 tablespoon white vinegar
2 1/2 teaspoons celery seed
1 cup vegetable oil

Whisk in a bowl or process in a food processor all ingredients, except the oil. Slowly beat in oil until dressing is emulsified. Makes 1 1/2 cups dressing.

ORANGE AND ALMOND SALAD
The Palliser

The Palliser has been a Truro landmark for four generations, offering guests a "home away from home" dining experience. The addition of grated peel and orange liqueur makes this a delightful salad, and we wonder, "Was home ever this good?"

1/4 cup olive oil
1 teaspoon sugar
1 tablespoon cider vinegar
2 teaspoons grated orange peel
4 tablespoons orange juice concentrated
4 tablespoons orange liqueur
assorted iceberg and romaine lettuce leaves to
    serve 6
1 small can mandarin orange segments, drained
1/4 cup slivered almonds

Mix together oil, sugar, vinegar, peel, juice and liqueur. Break up lettuce leaves and place in a large bowl. Pour sauce over and lightly toss. Garnish with mandarin slices and a sprinkle of slivered almonds. Serves 6.

HERBED GREEN OLIVE SALAD
The Compass Rose Inn, N.S.

In some Mediterranean countries it is considered a great welcoming gesture to offer your guests olives. Suzanne and Rodger Pike feature a piquant olive salad seasoned with herbs as a sign of their hospitality.

2 cups green olives, drained and halved
4 stalks celery, chopped
1 sweet red pepper, diced
1 small red onion, diced
1 carrot, diced small
1 garlic clove, chopped fine and mixed with
    1/4 teaspoon salt
2 teaspoons dried oregano
1/4 teaspoon hot red pepper flakes
2 tablespoons red wine vinegar
1/4 cup olive oil

Combine first six ingredients in a bowl and mix well. In another small bowl, whisk together remaining ingredients until well blended. Pour oil mixture over vegetables and toss, making sure all the vegetables are well coated. Refrigerate to combine flavours.

To serve, make a bed of lettuce leaves on individual salad plates and top with the olive mixture. Serves 6 to 8.

RED ONION DRESSING
The Cobequid Inn

Nancy Cleveland, owner–chef of the Cobequid Inn, says that this easy-to-prepare dressing is the perfect accompaniment to a salad of greens. Her guests are amused by the pale pink colour and rave about the flavour.

1/3 cup chopped red onion
1/3 cup white wine vinegar (can substitute
    with red wine vinegar)
1/3 cup sugar
1/4 teaspoon dry mustard
1/4 teaspoon salt
1 cup vegetable oil

Combine all ingredients in a blender and process until emulsified. This tart–sweet dressing is delicious on any combination of greens.

Souris, P.E.I.

COMPOSED FRUIT AND AVOCADO SALAD WITH CITRUS VINAIGRETTE
Duncreigan Country Inn of Mabou

Eleanor Mullendore's fruit salad can be served with a choice of dressings. The first is more decadent with the inclusion of salad oil. The second, Yoghurt and Orange Dressing, is for the health-conscious gourmet.

1/2 cup fresh orange juice
1/4 cup fresh grapefruit juice
1 tablespoon lemon juice
1 tablespoon honey (or to taste)
3/4 to 1 cup salad oil
lettuce leaves
grapefruit and orange segments, sliced
    avocado, cubed cantaloupe and
    strawberries to serve 6 (6 -8 cups)
poppy seeds

Combine juices and honey in a bowl and blend well. Slowly whisk in amount of oil needed to give desired thickness. Arrange lettuce on individual salad plates and top with fruit. Drizzle vinaigrette over fruit and sprinkle with poppy seeds. Serves 6.

Yoghurt and Orange Dressing
1 cup plain, low-fat yoghurt
1/4 cup frozen orange concentrate (undiluted)
1 tablespoon honey

Whisk all ingredients together until well blended. Serve with Composed Fruit Salad. Makes 1 1/4 cups.

MOROCCAN CHICKEN SALAD
Gaston's Restaurant

A meal in itself, Gaston's Moroccan Chicken Salad combines fresh herbs and vegetables with grilled chicken slices topped with a smooth, creamy dressing that features just a hint of mint. We had excellent results testing this recipe with low-fat ingredients.

4 small chicken breasts, skinless and boneless
1/4 cup mayonnaise
1/4 cup sour cream
1/4 cup plain yoghurt
2 tablespoons chopped fresh mint (1 1/2 teaspoons dried)
Bibb lettuce to serve 4
12 cherry tomatoes, cut in half
24 slices cucumber
1 small can mandarin oranges, drained
1/2 cup slivered almonds, toasted
4 sprigs fresh parsley, chopped

Grill chicken and leave to cool.
    Meanwhile, prepare dressing by whisking together mayonnaise, sour cream, yoghurt and mint; cover and refrigerate several hours to blend flavours.
    Thinly slice cooled chicken.
    Arrange lettuce leaves on 4 plates and top with dressing.
    Alternate tomato and cucumber at the edge of the plates and arrange chicken in a pinwheel pattern at the centre. Top with orange sections, toasted almonds and parsley. Serves 4

POTATO AND MUSSEL SALAD
Strathgartney Country Inn

Strathgartney is a warm and inviting inn, and it is fitting that the chef should prepare this innovative salad using fresh Prince Edward Island mussels and newly harvested potatoes.

1 1/2 to 2 pounds potatoes
3/4 cup olive oil
1/4 cup white wine vinegar
1/4 cup white wine
3 tablespoons fresh basil, chopped
Salt and freshly ground pepper, to taste

24 cultivated mussels, steamed and shucked
Fresh salad greens
8 cherry tomatoes
Edible flowers for garnish

Wash potatoes and boil until tender. Drain and let potatoes dry and begin to cool.
    Meanwhile, prepare vinaigrette. Combine oil, vinegar, wine, basil, salt and pepper in a blender and process until well blended.
    Peel and cut warm potatoes into 3/8-inch slices. Gently toss with half of the vinaigrette and cool to room temperature. Toss mussels with the remaining vinaigrette.
    To assemble, line plates with salad greens. Add a circle of potato slices, overlapping slightly. Arrange mussels in the centre of each plate with tomatoes. Garnish with flowers. Serves 4.

HONEY MUSTARD DRESSING
The Garrison House Inn

Honey and Dijon mustard are combined to produce a sweet yet tangy flavour in this delicious creamy dressing.

3 tablespoons raspberry vinegar
1 1/2 tablespoon honey
6 tablespoons mayonnaise
1 tablespoon Dijon mustard
1 tablespoon onion, minced
1 1/2 tablespoons fresh parsley, chopped
pinch of salt
3/4 cup oil (olive, vegetable or combination)

Combine all ingredients, except oil, in a blender. Add oil in a slow stream, processing only until blended. Yields 1 1/2 cups dressing.

Inn-on-the-Lake

MILFORD HOUSE SALAD DRESSING
Milford House

Guests keep coming back to Milford House because of its tradition of keeping the tried-and-true ways. Basic recipes of comfort food, like their House Salad Dressing, have been handed down over the decades.

1 tablespoon dry mustard
1/8 teaspoon celery salt
2 teaspoons sugar
1/4 teaspoon salt
1/4 teaspoon paprika
dash of pepper
1 tablespoon Worcestershire sauce
1/4 cup ketchup
1 clove crushed garlic
1/2 cup white vinegar
1 cup vegetable oil

Combine all ingredients, except oil, in a blender. Add oil in a slow stream, processing only until blended. Yields 2 cups.

WARM SEAFOOD AND CHICKEN SALAD
The Inn-on-the-Lake

Chef Roland Glauser combines sliced chicken, scallops, shrimps and fruit drizzled with his unique dressing for an excellent appetizer or luncheon choice.

2 chicken breasts, boneless and skinless
2 tablespoons butter
12 scallops
12 shrimps
1/4 cup white wine
2 tablespoons lime juice
2 tablespoons thick teriyaki sauce
1 teaspoon lime zest
1 orange, peeled and thinly sliced
1 apple, diced
2 tablespoons each red and green pepper, diced
lettuce to serve four
1/4 cup almond slivers, toasted

Cut chicken in strips and sauté in butter until almost done. Add seafood and sauté quickly. Add wine, lime juice, teriyaki sauce and zest; return to a boil and add orange, apple and peppers. Heat one minute and serve on a bed of lettuce. Garnish with toasted almonds. Serves 4.

Lobster Thermidor (Candleriggs)

SEAFOOD

It is not surprising to find that the cuisine of the Maritimes goes hand-in-hand with a tradition of seafood recipes. From the early days of European settlement, communities in the region have had the fishery as their cornerstone and their foundation, and, until recently, the abundance of fresh fish was a given. Haddock, salmon, lobster and scallops are just a few of the species most commonly relished in homes and restaurants. Today, it is difficult to believe that in the 1940s the children of lobster fishermen would rather have taken peanut butter sandwiches to school than those made from today's crustacean delicacy.

Maritimers love fresh seafood and visitors love to come and enjoy it with them. Unfortunately, the very source of their pleasure is at present in jeopardy with the drastic depletion of many species in the Atlantic coast fishery. We can only hope that with limitations on fishing quotas we will once again see an increase in stocks and be given a second chance to manage this valuable resource.

On a positive note, the decline in the fishery has seen the rise of consumer interest in less common species and an expansion in fish farming. The recipes we have collected from the chefs of our region reflect the diversity of seafood both wild and cultivated.

Seafood is often the quickest and easiest entrée to prepare. *Grilled Salmon with Lime Ginger and Pistachio Nut Vinaigrette* from Inverary Inn and *Haddock with Spanish Sauce* from the Bluenose Lodge require only minutes to cook the fish and slightly longer to prepare the sauces. Two recipes that can be prepared a few hours ahead of time include *Micmac Baked Haddock Fillets* from Salmon River House Country Inn and the *Inn Baked Halibut* from Amherst Shore Country Inn. Assemble, chill and remove from refrigerator 30 minutes before baking.

For an elegant presentation prepare *Cajun Spiced Salmon with Tomato Salsa and Roasted Seaweed* from Dalvay-by-the-Sea, or *Lobster Thermidor* from Candleriggs Restaurant. The extra time involved in preparation will be well worth the raves you receive from your guests.

Neils Harbour, Cape Breton, N.S.

LOBSTER SHANNON
Upper Deck Waterfront Fishery and Grill

Lobster is the most frequently requested seafood in Maritime restaurants! This recipe from Halifax's Upper Deck will be one to remember.

2 tablespoons butter
2 tablespoons flour
1 cup fish stock or reserved lobster juice
linguini or fettucini to serve 4
1/2 cup white wine
2 tablespoons lemon juice
1/4 teaspoon freshly crushed peppercorn
1 can frozen lobster meat (11.3 ounces)
1/2 cup heavy cream (35% m.f.)

Melt butter in a saucepan over low heat. Add flour, blending well. Whisk in stock. Bring to a boil, stirring until the first bubbles appear. Reduce the heat and cook 30 minutes, stirring frequently.

Prepare pasta according to package directions until *al dente*.

Mix together the wine, lemon juice, pepper and lobster in a large skillet. Quickly sauté until warmed, add sauce, heavy cream and cooked pasta. Simmer gently 3 to 4 minutes. Add salt and pepper to taste. Serves 4.

Lobster Shannon (Upper Deck Waterfront Fishery and Grill)

LOBSTER THERMIDOR
Candleriggs

This recipe makes an excellent choice for guests. It not only tastes delicious but can be prepared in advance and is impressive in its presentation.

water sufficient to boil lobsters
1 onion, chopped
1 celery stock, chopped
1 bay leaf
1 lemon, sliced
4 uncooked lobsters, 1 1/4 - 1 1/2 pounds each
2 tablespoons butter, melted
1/4 cup butter
2 tablespoons chopped chives
1/4 cup flour
2/3 cup blend (10% m.f.)
1/4 cup dry sherry
1/2 teaspoon dry mustard
salt and pepper to taste
1/2 cup soft breadcrumbs, ground fine
1/3 cup grated Swiss or Parmesan cheese
fresh parsley or dill for garnish

Pour water into a large pot and add onion, celery, bay leaf, and lemon slices. Bring to a boil and reduce heat to simmer for 10 minutes. Add lobsters and bring back to a boil. Skim off foam and simmer for 10 to 12 minutes. Remove lobsters, strain broth and reserve 1 cup.

Split lobster tails and bodies and cut lengthwise. Remove meat from tails, knuckles and claws and cut into pieces. Discard all shells except lobster bodies and tails. Clean shells under running water and brush inside and out with first amount of butter.

In a saucepan melt 1/4 cup of butter and sauté chives until tender. Stir in flour to make a roux and gradually whisk in blend and reserved broth, stirring over medium heat until thickened. Add sherry and mustard, cooking for one additional minute. Season with salt and pepper and stir in breadcrumbs and lobster chunks.

Place shells on a greased broiler pan and spoon the lobster mixture into them. Top with cheese and broil until golden and heated through, approximately 7 minutes. Garnish with fresh parsley or dill.

FRAGRANT AND TENDER SCALLOPS
The Matthew House Inn

Quickly and easily prepared, this Northern Italian version of sautéed scallops is colourful in its presentation and a delightfully flavourful dish.

2 cloves garlic, crushed
2 tablespoons chopped shallots
5 tablespoons extra virgin olive oil
salt to taste
1 pound fresh mushrooms, stems removed, and sliced thin
1/4 cup dry white wine
1 pound fresh scallops, cut in half if large
pinch dried hot red peppers
3/4 cup roasted sweet red peppers, cut into pieces*
1 cup fresh spinach, washed, dried and torn into pieces
2 tablespoons fresh basil, chopped
8 ounces linguini or spaghetti, cooked *al dente*
1/4 cup roasted pine nuts

In a heavy skillet, sauté garlic and shallots in oil until golden. Turn heat to medium and add a pinch of salt and the mushrooms. Sauté mushrooms 4 to 5 minutes, stirring occasionally and adding additional oil if needed. Stir in wine and simmer until evaporated — approximately 3 minutes. Add scallops, hot pepper, roasted red pepper, spinach and basil. Stir constantly over medium-high heat until scallops are cooked, about 4 minutes. Immediately toss with drained pasta. Garnish with sprigs of fresh basil and roasted pine nuts. Serves 4.

*Grill pepper until it is black on all sides. Place immediately in a brown paper bag until it is cooled. Peel the blackened skin and remove stocks and seeds.

Alma, N.B.

SCALLOP BUBBLY BAKE
The West Point Lighthouse

Cooks will find that this easily prepared seafood casserole, served with a delicate pasta or rice pilaf and accompanying side salad, is a well-balanced and nutritious meal.

1 pound scallops
2 tablespoons butter (for sautéing)
1/2 cup finely chopped onion
1 cup sliced mushrooms
1 cup chopped green pepper
1 cup celery, chopped
4 tablespoons butter (2nd amount)
4 tablespoons flour
1/2 teaspoon salt
2 cups milk
1/2 cup breadcrumbs
1 tablespoon butter
cheddar or Parmesan cheese, grated

Prepare scallops, cutting large ones in half. Poach scallops in boiling, salted water for 1 minute. Drain and set aside. Meanwhile, sauté onions, mushrooms, green pepper and celery in 2 tablespoons butter until onion is softened.

In a saucepan, melt 4 tablespoons butter (2nd amount) and whisk in flour and salt. Add milk, whisking constantly and cook until sauce is thickened and bubbly. Fold scallops and vegetables into the sauce and pour into a buttered 8-cup casserole. Top with breadcrumbs, dot with butter and a sprinkling of grated cheese. Bake in preheated 350°F oven for 25 to 30 minutes, until it is browned and bubbly. Serves 4.

The Manor Inn

COQUILLE ST. JACQUES
The Manor Inn

Served in individual scallop shells surrounded by potato rosettes, the Manor Inn's version of this classic French dish is attractive and simple to prepare.

1 1/2 pound fresh scallops
2 tablespoons butter
2 tablespoons lemon juice
2 green onions, sliced
6 medium mushrooms, sliced
2 tablespoons butter (2nd amount)
1/2 cup white wine
1 cup medium white sauce
salt and pepper, to taste
4 medium potatoes, boiled and whipped
1/2 cup grated mozzarella cheese
lemon wedges and parsley springs for garnish

Sauté scallops in butter about 2 minutes. Add lemon juice and remove from skillet to a bowl.
Sauté onions and mushrooms in second amount of butter for two minutes, add wine and liquid from scallops. Bring to a boil and reduce by one third.

Prepare **white sauce** and blend into mushroom mixture; season to taste with salt and pepper.
To serve, place scallops in four large baking shells or a shallow casserole. Pour sauce over scallops, pipe whipped potatoes around seafood and sprinkle with cheese. Broil 4 inches from heat source until bubbly and slightly browned. Yields 4 to 6 servings.

White Sauce
2 tablespoons butter
2 tablespoons flour
1 cup milk

Heat butter in a small saucepan over medium heat, whisk in flour and cook roux 2 to 3 minutes until bubbling. Add milk all at once, and cook quickly stirring constantly till mixture thickens and bubbles.

SCALLOPS VERT-PRÉS
Chez Françoise

Chef Jacques Cadieux Johnny uses large Digby scallops and fresh chives and leeks to prepare this simple dish. He suggests serving it with a rice pilaf or Duchess potatoes.

1 pound fresh scallops
1/2 cup garlic butter
1/4 cup chopped green onion or chives
1/2 cup chopped leek, white and green parts
1/2 cup dry white wine
freshly ground pepper

Melt butter in a large skillet over medium heat. Add scallops and sauté slowly, turning once. Add green onion, leek and wine, continuing to cook until scallops are just cooked and wine-vegetable mixture resembles a light sauce. Season with freshly ground pepper. Serves 4.

Chez Françoise

JUMBO SHRIMP MCCRADY
McCrady's Green Acres

A hint of Pernod flavours this delightful mouth-watering dish. At McCrady's, the shrimps and colourful vegetables are served over rice.

1 1/2 to 2 pounds jumbo shrimp, shelled and deveined
2 tablespoons garlic butter
4 tablespoons Pernod
1/2 each red and green peppers, in julienne strips
1 cup of **Hollandaise sauce** page 71

Sauté prepared shrimp in garlic butter until just pink. Flambé with pernod, and set aside. Prepare Hollandaise sauce and add shrimp and julienne of peppers. Yields 4 servings.

BOMBAY SHRIMP
Nemo's Restaurant

Nemo's owner, Brian Trainor, who developed this shrimp recipe, tells us that the vinaigrette is delicious as a dressing for a cold seafood salad!

1 tablespoon vegetable oil
1 1/2 pounds uncooked large shrimp, peeled and deveined
1/4 cup sweet mango chutney
1/4 cup white wine
1/4 cup mango purée, fresh or canned
3/4 cup Curried Almond Vinaigrette (see below)
assorted fresh fruit and lettuce leaves, for garnish
2 tablespoons mango chutney

Heat oil in a large skillet until oil forms ribbons, Add shrimp and cook 30 seconds per side or until almost done. Remove shrimp to a bowl and wipe pan with a paper towel.

Return shrimp to pan and add 1/4 cup of chutney, wine, mango purée and curried almond vinaigrette. Simmer gently, stirring until ingredients are blended and shrimp and sauce are at serving temperature. To serve, divide between four plates and garnish with lettuce, fresh fruit, such as mango, melon slices, kiwi slices, or berries, and 1 tablespoon of chutney.

Curried Almond Vinaigrette
2/3 cup vegetable oil
4 tablespoons white vinegar
2 tablespoons crushed almonds
sprig of fresh parsley, chopped
1 teaspoon curry, or to taste
1 1/2 teaspoon onion, puréed
pinch of sugar
salt and pepper, to taste

Prepare vinaigrette by combining oil, vinegar, almonds, parsley, curry, onion and sugar in a saucepan and simmer 20 minutes, stirring occasionally. Season with salt and pepper and set aside to cool. Shake well before adding to shrimp.

MICMAC BAKED HADDOCK FILLETS
Salmon River House Country Inn

It is said that pioneers learned to bake fish from the local Indians who wrapped their catch in wet leaves with a combination of herbs, fruits and roots, then baked it in a fire. Adrien Blanchette, owner of the Salmon River House Country Inn, jokingly comments that he substitutes foil for wet leaves.

1 1/2 pounds haddock fillets
8 slices of apple
8 thin slices of onion
8 slices of lemon
8 slices of tomato
2 teaspoons butter
summer savory
salt and pepper to taste

Prepare the fillets by carefully removing bones. Cut fillets into 4 portions and place each on a large square of tinfoil. Alternate slices of apple, onion, lemon and tomato on each fillet and dot with butter. Season with a pinch of summer savory, salt and pepper.

Enclose fillets in the foil, being careful to seal all edges. Bake in a preheated 325°F oven for approximately 20 to 25 minutes, depending on the thickness of the fish. Serve by folding back the foil to form a boat that retains the juices. Serves 4.

West Dover, N.S.

HADDOCK WITH SPANISH SAUCE
Bluenose Lodge

The owners of Bluenose Lodge say that this is an excellent buffet dish as the sauce prevents the fish from drying out. If cooking for a buffet, leave the fillets whole and arrange on a large oval plate, napped with Spanish Sauce and garnished with fresh parsley.

1 pound fresh haddock fillets
1/4 cup flour
1/4 teaspoon salt
1/4 teaspoon pepper
1 tablespoon finely chopped fresh parsley
1/2 teaspoon paprika
1 tablespoon canola oil
Spanish Sauce

Remove any bones from the haddock and cut in serving-size pieces. Combine flour, salt, pepper, parsley and paprika and mix well. Dredge fish in flour. Heat oil in a skillet and quickly sauté haddock, turning once. Fish is cooked when it flakes easily and is opaque. Top haddock with Spanish Sauce. Serves 4.

Spanish Sauce
1 can tomatoes (14 ounces)
1 small onion, coarsely chopped
1 stalk celery, coarsely chopped
1 small green pepper, coarsely chopped
1 shake tabasco
1/2 teaspoon freshly ground black pepper
1 1/2 tablespoons fresh parsley, chopped

Combine all ingredients in a heavy-bottomed saucepan and cook over low heat for one hour or until thick. Break up tomatoes as the sauce simmers and stir often as it will burn easily. Yields 2 cups.

Halibut and Shitake Mushrooms Baked in Rice Paper (Tattingstone Inn)

POACHED HADDOCK BRAEMAR
Candleriggs

Candleriggs owner Jean Cochrane prepares a menu to reflect a blending of Old and New Scotland. Haddock Braemar is easy to prepare and can be served with a sauce or herbed butter. The chef serves it with rice pilaf and fresh vegetables, garnished with a julienne of carrots, scallions and black olives.

2 pounds fresh haddock fillets

6 sea scallops
6 medium shrimps, shelled and deveined

Dressing
2 cups fresh breadcrumbs, finely grated
1/4 cup finely chopped pimentos
1/4 cup finely chopped onion
1/4 cup finely chopped green pepper
1/4 cup finely chopped celery
salt and pepper
pinch of sweet basil

Slice fillets down the centre and divide into 6 portions. Grease individual ramekins with butter and line dishes with fillets. Place 1 scallop and 1 shrimp in the center of each dish and set aside. Prepare dressing by combining breadcrumbs, pimento, onion, green pepper, celery, salt, pepper and basil, and moisten with 1 teaspoon of water, if desired. Divide dressing between dishes and place on top of seafood. Cover each dish with a piece of waxed paper, and tie in place.

Pour an inch of water in an electric skillet and bring to a boil. Place ramekins in the skillet and reduce heat. Replace cover and steam cook for 12 to 14 minutes. To serve, remove waxed paper and invert onto serving plates. Serves 6.

THE INN BAKED HALIBUT
Amherst Shore Country Inn

Donna and Jim Laceby have an extensive garden at their inn on the Amherst Shore. This baked halibut entrée goes nicely with crisp, fresh spring vegetables, such as asparagus or baby carrots.

1 1/2 pounds halibut fillets
12 ounces plain cream cheese*
1 tablespoon dry onion soup mix
1 1/2 teaspoons dried tarragon
1 1/2 teaspoons Dijon style mustard
4 teaspoons blend (18% m.f.)
1 1/2 cups coarse fresh breadcrumbs
1 cup fresh parsley, finely chopped
1/2 cup grated Parmesan cheese

Place a large sheet of foil on a cookie sheet and grease generously. Place halibut fillets on foil and set aside.

Cream together the cream cheese, soup mix, tarragon, mustard and blend. Spread over top of fillets and bake in a preheated 475°F oven for 10 to 12 minutes.

Combine breadcrumbs, parsley and Parmesan cheese. Remove fish from oven and sprinkle with breadcrumb mixture. Return to oven and bake an additional 2 to 3 minutes until crumbs are browned and fish is cooked. Serves 6.

*This recipe was also tested using 'light' cream cheese and milk and the results was equally as delicious!

HALIBUT AND SHITAKE MUSHROOMS BAKED IN RICE PAPER
Tattingstone Inn

Chef Stephen Riley of Tattingstone suggests this colourful dish be served with a green vegetable, such as broccoli, and a brown and wild rice pilaf.

4 halibut filets (5 to 6 ounces each)
2 tablespoons butter
2 ounces dried shitake mushrooms*, soaked
    2 to 3 hours, drained and sliced
4 medium tomatoes, blanched, skinned, seeded
    and diced
1 tablespoon sweet basil or 1 teaspoon dry
4 sheets rice paper*

Melt 1 tablespoon of the butter in a skillet and sauté halibut on both sides, season with salt and pepper, set aside to cool.

Sauté prepared tomatoes, mushrooms and basil in remaining butter. Let cool.

Soak rice paper in lukewarm water until flexible, about 1 minute.

Place a sheet of rice paper on worktable. Place 1/4 of the tomato-mushroom mixture in the center, add the halibut. Fold the rice paper to form a package and place seam side down in a shallow baking dish. Prepare remaining fillets in the same manner. Bake 15 to 20 minutes, until paper is crispy.

To serve, place a rice package on each plate, top with Beurre Blanc Sauce. Serves 4.

*Shitake mushrooms and rice paper are available at specialty food stores.

Beurre Blanc Sauce
1 lemon, thinly sliced
1 tablespoon water
1/2 cup butter, melted

Sear lemon slices in a heated skillet for a few seconds. Add water and then the butter in a slow stream. Do not boil. Serve over each rice package.

Dalvay-by-the-Sea

HALIBUT WITH MUSHROOMS, TOMATOES AND ARTICHOKES
The Compass Rose Inn, N.S.

Cooks love to prepare halibut with its firm white flesh and mild flavour. The addition of mushrooms, fresh tomatoes and artichokes in this recipe give it a little extra flare.

4 halibut steaks or fillets
juice of 1 lemon
4 tablespoons butter
2 cups sliced mushrooms
4 artichoke hearts, quartered
2 cups peeled and diced tomatoes
1/3 cup parsley, chopped
1/2 cup prepared demi-glace (brown sauce)

Sprinkle halibut with lemon juice. In a skillet, heat 2 tablespoons of the butter and fry the halibut until just cooked, approximately 7 to 10 minutes depending upon thickness of fish. Fish is cooked when it flakes easily and is opaque. (Halibut may be grilled without butter.)

In a separate skillet, sauté mushrooms and artichokes in the remaining 2 tablespoons of butter. Add the tomatoes, demi-glace and parsley to the skillet and simmer for about 5 minutes. To serve, arrange halibut on plates and top with sauce. Serves 4.

SOLE ALMADINE
Auberge Le Heron Country Inn

At the Heron Country Inn fresh seafood is readily available. However, this recipe adapts well to any frozen white-fish fillets.

1 pound fresh sole fillets
3 tablespoons butter, melted
pinch of salt, pepper, and paprika
2 tablespoons butter
1 1/2 tablespoons lemon juice
1/4 cup blanched almonds
fresh chopped parsley to garnish

Place fillets in a single layer on a well-greased baking dish. Brush fillets with melted butter. Broil approximately 4 inches from heat for 10 minutes, or until fish flakes easily. Sprinkle cooked fillets with seasonings.

Prepare sauce while fish is cooking. Melt butter in a saucepan over low heat. Add lemon juice and almonds, stirring constantly.

Pour sauce over cooked fillets and garnish with chopped parsley. Yields 4 servings.

Cajun Spiced Salmon with Tomato Salsa and Roasted Seaweed
Dalvay-by-the-Sea

There may be some that say, the delicate taste of Atlantic salmon is perfect and does not need additions, but to Chef Richard Kemp, creation in the kitchen and presentation at your table is what makes a memorable meal. Under his guidance, Atlantic salmon is transformed into a spicy taste sensation with wonderful success.

Tomato Salsa
6 firm tomatoes, peeled, seeded and finely
    chopped
1 small Spanish onion, finely chopped
1 teaspoon each, coriander, basil, chives,
    chopped
1 teaspoon garlic, crushed
1 teaspoon Dijon mustard
3 teaspoons red wine vinegar
3 teaspoons balsamic vinegar
2 tablespoons olive oil
salt and pepper to taste

Combine tomatoes and onion in a bowl and mix well. Whisk together remaining seven ingredients until they are emulsified. Pour over tomatoes and stir well. Cover and refrigerate to let flavours combine.

Digby Pines golf course

Cajun Salmon
4 fillets of salmon or salmon steaks
1/4 to 1/2 cup Cajun spice mix*
1/4 cup clarified butter
1 sheet roasted *Nori* seaweed*, cut in thin strips

Dredge salmon fillets in the Cajun spices. Heat a heavy skillet (authors used cast-iron skillet directly on coals of barbecue) until very hot and smoking. Put salmon fillets in dry pan and add enough butter to moisten fish. Pan may flame so be careful. Quickly turn salmon to sear other side. Remove at once and place skillet in a preheated 400°F oven. Cook for approximately 5 to 7 minutes or until fish flakes and is opaque, being careful not to overcook.

To serve, place salmon on warmed plates and surround each fillet with tomato salsa. Make 4 nests with the strips of roasted seaweed and place on top of each fillet. Serves 4.

* Cajun spice mix and roasted nori seaweed are found in most Asian markets or specialty food stores.

Salmon fishing, Stewiacke River, N.S.

POACHED SALMON WITH MUSCAT
The Pines Resort Hotel

Executive Chef Claude AuCoin tells us that with the sweetness of wine and orange juice, salmon has a particularly delicate flavour. He recommends serving this dish with rice or fresh pasta, along with fresh vegetables, such as asparagus, peas or green beans.

4 fresh salmon fillets, 6 ounces each
1/2 cup muscat sweet wine
1/2 cup fish stock
1/2 cup fresh orange juice
1/2 cup heavy cream (35% m.f.)
salt and pepper

Simmer salmon in wine, stock and orange juice until cooked, approximately 5 to 7 minutes. Remove fish to a warm plate and reserve stock.

To finish sauce, boil stock to reduce by half. Incorporate the cream and reduce by half again. Season with salt and pepper. Serves 4.

SMOKED SALMON PASTA
Liscombe Lodge

Liscombe Lodge, situated on the banks of the Liscomb River, is famous for its salmon dishes. The chefs smoke fresh salmon naturally over wood and the result is delicious.

3 tablespoons butter
1 tablespoon minced onion
1 tablespoon each, diced red and green pepper
1 garlic clove, minced
1/2 pound smoked salmon, sliced in thin strips
2 tablespoons dry white vermouth
1/2 cup heavy cream (35% m.f.)
1/4 cup fresh parsley, chopped
3/4 pound pasta of choice, capellini, fettucini or other

In a skillet, melt butter and sauté onion, peppers and garlic until soft but not brown. Add salmon, stir and cook for one minute, Stir in vermouth, increase heat to medium and cook one minute. Stir in cream and half of the parsley and simmer a few minutes until sauce is slightly thickened.

Meanwhile, in a large pot of boiling water, cook pasta according to package directions until *al dente*. Drain pasta and toss with smoked salmon sauce. Garnish with remaining chopped parsley. Serves 4.

ITALIAN SEAFOOD CIOPPINO
Inverary Inn

Chef Mark Gabrieau enjoys the quiet lifestyle of Baddeck. He also loves the availability of fresh seafood and vegetables used to prepare this tasty seafood cioppino which he serves over rice or pasta.

1/4 cup olive oil
2 tablespoons diced onion
1/4 yellow pepper, in julienne strips
1/4 green pepper, in julienne strips
2 teaspoons fresh garlic, chopped fine
1 tablespoon sugar
2 teaspoons dried oregano
1/2 teaspoon black pepper
1 bay leaf
1 1/2 pound fresh tomatoes, peeled, seeded and diced
1 1/2 cup white wine
8 shrimp, shelled and deveined
8 large scallops
16 fresh mussels
8 ounces fresh salmon fillet, in chunks
1 lobster (1 pound), cooked, shelled and cut in chunks

Heat oil in a heavy pot over medium high heat. Add onion, yellow and green peppers, garlic, sugar, oregano, pepper and bay leaf. Sauté two minutes. Add tomatoes and wine. Bring to a boil and add shrimp, scallops, mussels, salmon and lobster meat. Simmer until fish is cooked and mussel shells are open. Spoon over rice or buttered pasta. Serves 4.

Entrance to the Normaway Inn

Margaree River sport fishing

GRILLED SALMON WITH SAGE BUTTER
The Normaway Inn

Chef Ryan Nicholson states that Atlantic salmon grills better and has a more fragrant flavour than Pacific salmon due to its higher fat content. He also suggests that the tail section of a salmon is preferred for grilling, while the mid section is better for poaching.

1/2 cup onion, diced
1/2 teaspoon butter
1/2 cup fresh sage leaves
dash of salt and pepper
1/8 teaspoon lemon juice
1 cup unsalted butter, in cubes
4 to 6 salmon fillets, unskinned (4 to 6 ounces each)

In a skillet, slowly sauté onion in butter until brown. Remove to a fine mesh strainer and drain for 1 hour. In a food processor, combine onion and sage leaves and process until leaves are chopped. Add salt, pepper, lemon juice and butter, one cube at a time and process until smooth.

Reserve 1/3 cup of sage butter for salmon and roll out remainder of butter in a tubelike fashion, on cellowrap. Roll up and seal ends. This may be frozen and portions broken off to use with fish, meats or vegetables. Makes 1 cup.

Grill salmon fillets on flesh side for approximately 6 to 7 minutes, flip over to skin side and cook 2 to 3 minutes until fish flakes easily and is opaque. To serve, remove skin from fillets and dress with sage butter. Serves 4 to 6.

Combine all ingredients, except salmon, and whisk until they are emulsified. Gently warm vinaigrette while preparing salmon.

Grill salmon steaks until they flake easily and are opaque, approximately 7 to 10 minutes depending on thickness of fish. To serve, pour warm vinaigrette over salmon. Serves 4 to 6.

OFFERINGS OF THE ATLANTIC
Parkerhouse Inn

The Parkerhouse Inn in downtown Saint John is located a stone's throw from the bay. It is fitting that this house speciality should include a variety of Atlantic seafoods complimented by a smooth garlic and dill sauce.

2 cups of water
2 bay leaves
8 peppercorns
2 large sprigs of parsley
1/2 teaspoon salt
3 tablespoons white wine
4 salmon fillets, 4 ounces each
8 large scallops
16 to 20 mussels
12 jumbo shrimp, peeled and deveined
Garlic Dill Sauce

Place first 6 ingredients in a large skillet and bring to a boil. Immerse all fish in poaching liquid. Cover and let cook about 5 minutes or until mussels open and fish is tender. Remove fish to a plate and keep warm. Strain poaching liquid into a 2-cup measure and reserve for Garlic Dill Sauce.

Divide seafood between four plates and serve with Garlic Dill Sauce. Garnish with fresh dill.

Garlic Dill Sauce
1/2 cup heavy cream (35% m.f.)
1/2 teaspoon white pepper
1 teaspoon minced garlic, or to taste
1 tablespoon fresh dill, chopped
2 cups reserved poaching liquid
2 tablespoons roux formed by kneading together
    2 tablespoons flour and 2 1/2 tablespoons of
    butter, and formed into small balls
salt to taste

Parkerhouse Inn

GRILLED SALMON WITH LIME, GINGER AND PISTACHIO NUT VINAIGRETTE
Inverary Inn

Chef Mark Gabrieau at the Inverary Inn suggests that the Lime, Ginger and Pistachio Nut Vinaigrette *served with this salmon dish is delicious on a variety of grilled seafoods.*

1/2 cup olive oil
1/4 cup white-wine vinegar
1/4 cup pistachio nuts, crushed
zest and juice of 2 limes
zest and juice of 1 orange
1 tablespoon fresh ginger, minced
1 teaspoon peppercorns
1/2 teaspoon fresh tarragon, chopped
1 teaspoon shallots, minced
1 teaspoon fresh parsley, chopped
1 teaspoon Worcestershire sauce
pinch of salt and pepper
4 to 6 salmon steaks or fillets

Inverary Inn

Heat cream, pepper, garlic, dill and reserved poaching liquid in a heavy saucepan and bring to a boil. Reduce slightly and add roux balls one at a time until sauce has reached desired thickness. Serves 4.

ROAST SALMON WITH RED WINE, BACON AND VEGETABLE MIREPOIX
Cooper's Inn and Restaurant

At Cooper's Inn the Hynes take great care in preparing their unique recipes. The roast salmon and sauce are examples of the chef's ingenuity and have become a house speciality.

4 strips of bacon, diced
1 carrot
1 leek
1 celery stick
4 salmon fillets, 6 ounces each
salt and pepper, to taste
1/2 cup chicken stock
1/4 cup red wine
1 teaspoon fresh thyme, chopped (1/4 teaspoon dried)
1/2 tablespoon flour
2 teaspoons unsalted butter

Preheat oven to 450°F. Fry bacon in a heavy skillet to remove fat and set aside. Make a *mirepoix* of the vegetables by finely dicing carrots, leek and celery to uniform cubes. Simmer vegetables until crisp tender and place a spoonful of vegetables on top of each fillet in an oiled baking pan. Roast in the oven until the center of the salmon is just pink, approximately 10 minutes.

While salmon is baking combine the stock, wine and thyme and bring to a boil. Reduce this by one half. Prepare a roux by kneading together the flour and butter, forming small balls. Add roux balls, one at a time to simmering sauce until it has reached the consistency of heavy cream. Add the diced bacon and serve over fillets. Serves 4.

Chicken Supreme (The Captain's House)

ENTRÉES

Whether you prefer wholesome meat and potato dishes or innovative pasta creations, there is something for everyone in this cookbook.

Chefs from over sixty establishments have welcomed us into their kitchens and generously shared their specialities. The following section includes a sampling of their preparations for poultry, lamb, beef and pork, together with a variety of pasta and lighter vegetarian creations.

We are often asked, "What is your favourite dish?", and "How do you choose the recipes?" We can tell you that the innkeepers and chefs usually offer what they feel best reflects the quality and style of their establishments and we have never been disappointed.

In sampling the fine fare offered throughout the Maritimes, we found many recipes suitable for family-style meals and others that could be used for elegant entertaining. We offer several ways to prepare boneless chicken breasts in this section, many suitable for a novice cook. Spring lamb, a speciality of Cape Breton and Prince Edward Island, is featured in several recipes. Since beef and pork are popular restaurant choices, a few innovative recipes have been included.

We hope that with our directions, you will have the confidence to create these dishes in your own kitchens. *Bon appetit!*

The Captain's House

CHICKEN SUPREME
The Captain's House

Nicki Butler of the Captain's House tells us that to respect patrons' dietary needs, they serve the Sherry Cream Sauce in a small dish on the side.

4 boneless, skinless chicken breasts (6 ounces)
1/2 pound mushrooms, chopped
1/2 cup finely chopped onion
1 clove garlic, minced
2 tablespoons olive oil
salt and pepper to taste

With a very sharp knife, cut into the underside of each chicken breast to form a pocket. Reserve breasts. In a skillet, heat 1 tablespoon of the olive oil and sauté mushrooms, garlic and onion until soft. Season with salt and pepper to taste.
   Stuff the mushroom mixture into the pockets of the chicken breasts and turn over. Add remaining 1 tablespoon of oil to the skillet and over moderate heat, quickly seal and brown the breasts all over. Transfer the breasts, pocket side down, to a shallow casserole and bake in a preheated 350°F oven for 20 minutes. Serve breasts with **Sherry cream sauce**. Serves 4.

Sherry cream sauce
2/3 cup heavy cream (32% m.f.)
2 tablespoons butter
2 tablespoons sweet sherry
1/2 teaspoon cornstarch dissolved in 1 teaspoon cold water
salt and pepper

Whisk cream, butter and sherry in a small saucepan over high heat.
   Gradually whisk in cornstarch and stir until slightly thickened. Season with salt and pepper to taste. Makes 3/4 cup sauce.

CHICKEN BREASTS EXOTIC
The Inn-on-the-Lake

The chef at the Inn-on-the-Lake suggests serving this exotic chicken dish with steamed vegetables and rice pilaf.

4 boneless chicken breasts, 6 ounces each
1/2 apple, diced
1 plum, diced
1 kiwi, diced
2/3 banana, diced
8 pieces pineapple, diced
1 1/2 tablespoons mango chutney
1 tablespoon vegetable oil for browning
1/2 cup plain yoghurt
1/4 teaspoon curry (or to taste)
dash of salt and pepper

Prepare chicken by slicing a pocket in the side of each breast being careful not to cut all the way through. Toss fruit and chutney together and divide between breast pockets. Add oil to skillet and brown breasts 3 minutes per side. Transfer to a baking dish and bake at 350°F until cooked, approximately 15 to 20 minutes.
   Combine yoghurt, curry and seasoning and spoon over cooked chicken. Serves 4.

The Captain's House

65

Parkerhouse Inn

CHICKEN IN FILO PASTRY
Parkerhouse Inn

This chicken entrée may take a little longer to prepare but the enjoyment it will bring your guests is worth the effort. Lobster may be substituted for shrimp in the stuffing with the same delicious results.

1/4 cup butter
2 green onions, chopped
1 garlic clove, minced
3/4 pound cooked shrimp, coarsely chopped
1 teaspoon flour
1 tablespoon white, dry vermouth
1 tablespoon brandy
1/4 cup heavy cream (32% m.f.)
4 boneless, chicken breasts (6 ounces each)
salt and pepper to season
8 sheets filo pastry
melted butter
1 cup chicken stock
1 small garlic clove, crushed
1 tablespoon cornstarch
1 tablespoon fresh parsley, chopped
white pepper to taste

Heat half the butter in a skillet and sauté green onions and garlic for 1 minute. Add shrimp and cook for 30 seconds. In a bowl, whisk flour into the vermouth. Add brandy, and cream, and stir this mixture into the skillet with the shrimp. When thickened, remove from heat and cool.

Cut a large slit in the side of each chicken breast to form a pocket, being careful not to cut through. Season inside of pockets with salt and pepper. Stuff breasts with seafood mixture. Heat remaining butter in a skillet and sauté breasts, turning carefully, until they are almost cooked. About 3 minutes each side.

Brush 2 sheets of filo pastry with melted butter and layer one on top of the other. Place breast at one end of filo, fold in sides and roll to form a package. Repeat. Place breasts on a buttered baking sheet and bake in a preheated 350°F oven for 15 minutes.

To prepare garlic sauce bring chicken stock and crushed garlic clove to a boil. Dissolve cornstarch in 1 tablespoon of water and quickly whisk into the stock. Stir until thickened, add parsley and season with pepper.

Serve chicken packages topped with garlic sauce. Serves 4.

GRILLED BREAST OF CHICKEN WITH APPLE BRANDY SAUCE
Halliburton House Inn

We are sure this succulent chicken dish will become a favourite in your recipe collection. We tested the sauce using Calvados brandy with excellent results.

1/2 regular onion, chopped
1 clove garlic, chopped
1 cup apple juice
1 1/2 cups heavy cream (32% m.f.)
1 tablespoon brandy
1/2 apple, diced
salt and pepper to taste
4 boneless, skinless chicken breasts (6 ounces each)

In saucepan over medium heat, combine onion, garlic and apple juice. Bring to a boil and reduce volume by three-quarters. Add cream and reduce volume by half. Press through a fine strainer, add brandy and apples. Adjust seasoning with salt and pepper.

Grill chicken breasts on a barbecue or electric grill, approximately 5 minutes per side, being careful not to overcook. Serve with sauce. Yields 4 servings.

LOON BAY LODGE CHICKEN VERONIQUE
Loon Bay Lodge

We asked the management of Loon Bay Lodge for a "health conscious" chicken dish. Not only does their Chicken Veronique fill the request, it is delicious.

4 chicken breasts, boneless and skinless
1 cup cracker crumbs
1/4 teaspoon black pepper
1/2 teaspoon dried tarragon
pinch of nutmeg
3 tablespoons butter
1/4 cup chopped onion
2 cups sliced mushrooms
1/2 cup chicken broth
1/2 cup white wine
2 cups seedless green grapes

Combine crumbs, pepper, tarragon and nutmeg and coat chicken breasts. Melt butter and brown chicken on both sides. Transfer to a shallow baking dish.

Add onion and mushrooms to skillet and sauté until tender. Deglaze pan with broth and wine. Pour over chicken and bake, uncovered at 375°F for 20 to 25 minutes. Add grapes to chicken and continue to bake until chicken is no longer pink in the centre, approximately 5 more minutes. Serves 4.

HEAVENLY CHICKEN
The Innlet Café

The chef tells us that the Innlet Café serves this delightful dish in individual casseroles accompanied by rice pilaf and green salad.

8 to 10 medium mushrooms, sliced
1/4 cup shallots, chopped
2 tablespoons butter, melted
1/2 cup white wine
3/4 cup water
3/4 cup heavy cream (32% m.f.)
1/2 cup sour cream
1 1/2 tablespoons soya sauce
1/4 cup butter
1/4 cup flour
1 teaspoon paprika
2 1/2 to 3 cups cooked chicken, in bite-size pieces

Prepare mushrooms and shallots and sauté in butter in a large skillet for a few minutes until wilted. Remove vegetables to a bowl and wipe pan clean. In a saucepan combine wine, water, cream, sour cream and soya sauce. Bring to a boil, reduce heat and simmer.

Melt second amount of butter (1/4 cup) in skillet, and whisk in flour and paprika. Cook roux one minute and remove from heat. Slowly add boiling wine-cream mixture, whisking constantly to prevent lumps forming. Fold in cooked chicken and vegetables. Serve immediately or reheat at 350°F for 20 to 30 minutes. Serves 4 to 6.

The Compass Rose Inn, Lunenburg, N.S.

CHICKEN VERONIQUE
The Compass Rose Inn, N.S.

Boneless chicken breasts are a chef's delight; easy to prepare and quick to cook. The green grapes, creamy sauce and hint of herbs in this chicken dish is popular with guests as well.

1/2 teaspoon oregano, dried
1/2 teaspoon thyme, dried
6 deboned chicken breasts
2 tablespoons butter
1 garlic clove, crushed
2 to 3 dozen seedless, green grapes, halved
1/2 cup white wine
1/2 cup heavy cream (32% mf)

Crumble thyme and oregano together and pat into both sides of chicken breasts. In a skillet melt butter and garlic and sauté breasts until browned, and cooked, about 5 minutes on each side. Remove breasts and keep warm.

Deglaze skillet with wine, scraping up the brown sediment. Add cream and simmer until the sauce is thickened. Add grapes to sauce during last few minutes, to heat through. Pour sauce over chicken to serve. Serves 4 to 6.

SICILIAN CHICKEN
Bluenose Lodge

Ron and Grace Swan of the Bluenose Lodge make an effort to feature healthy dishes on their menu. Sicilian Chicken is a fine example of their ability to provide low-fat cuisine that looks and tastes great.

4 boneless chicken breasts (6 ounces each)
1/4 cup flour
1/4 teaspoon salt
1/4 teaspoon pepper
1 tablespoon fresh parsley, chopped
1/2 teaspoon paprika
1/4 teaspoon dried oregano
1 tablespoon vegetable oil (chef uses canola)
8 slices fresh orange
3/4 cup fresh orange juice
1/4 cup sweet vermouth

Make a seasoned flour by combining flour, salt, pepper, parsley, paprika and oregano. Dredge chicken breasts in the seasoned flour. Heat oil in a skillet and add breasts, sautéing on both sides until golden and almost cooked. Cover each breast with 2 slices of orange and add orange juice. Cover and cook another few minutes. Remove breasts from skillet and keep warm.

Uncover skillet and reduce liquid to about 1/3 cup. Add vermouth and reduce slightly. Serve chicken with cooked orange slices or with fresh ones, if you prefer, topped with the orange-vermouth sauce. Serves 4.

THE AMHERST SHORE CHICKEN MARQUIS
Amherst Shore Country Inn

Donna Laceby allows the first guests to reserve a table the opportunity to help prepare the evening menu. Her Chicken Marquis is an all-time favourite.

4 skinless and deboned chicken breasts (5 to 6 ounces each)
salt and pepper, to taste
2 small cloves garlic, crushed
2 cups blanched spinach
4 1/2 ounces Brie or Camembert cheese
4 slices lean bacon, partially cooked
2 tablespoons butter, melted

Remove all fat from chicken breasts, rinse and pat dry. Place breasts between two sheets of waxed paper and pound with a meat mallet until they are slightly flattened and of a uniform thickness.

Sprinkle chicken with salt and pepper. Spread garlic on each breast. Top each one with 1/2 cup spinach which has been squeezed to remove moisture, and cheese. Roll up chicken breast and wrap with bacon. Place seam side down in a shallow baking dish. Brush with melted butter and bake in a preheated 350°F oven for 45 to 50 minutes, basting several times with pan juices and melted butter. Serves 4.

Haying near Stewiacke, N.S.

CHICKEN AND PEACHES
The Palliser

We just love a dish that is easily prepared, popped in the oven and ready to eat within the hour. We served Chicken and Peaches with hot steamy rice, homebaked rolls and a crisp side salad. The memory makes our mouths water!

2 tablespoons flour
1/2 teaspoon salt
1/2 teaspoon paprika
4 to 6 chicken breasts, trimmed and skin
    removed
1/2 cup peach jam
1/3 cup water
1/4 cup barbecue sauce
1/4 cup onions, diced
1/4 cup green pepper, diced
1 tablespoon soya sauce
1/3 cup water chestnuts, sliced
1 cup peaches, sliced

Combine flour, salt and paprika. Dredge chicken in flour mixture and lay pieces in a large shallow casserole. In a bowl, combine jam, water, barbecue sauce, onions, green pepper and soya sauce, and pour over chicken breasts. Bake, uncovered, in a preheated 350°F oven for 40 to 45 minutes, basting occasionally. Add peach slices and water chestnuts and bake for an additional 10 minutes, basting once or twice to make sure that peaches are glazed with sauce. Serves 4 to 6.

CHICKEN OSCAR
La Poissonnière Restaurant

We suggest you prepare the Hollandaise sauce for the Chicken Oscar as close to serving time as possible. This make a very attractive entrée — bright green asparagus, golden sauce, pink crab and browned breast, served with potatoes or rice.

5 tablespoons white wine vinegar
4 tablespoons water
1/2 teaspoon crushed white peppercorns
1 bay leaf
4 egg yolks
1/2 pound unsalted butter
pinch of salt and cayenne pepper
6 boneless, skinless chicken breasts, 5 ounces
    each
1 to 2 tablespoons light vegetable oil
12 asparagus spears
12 ounces crab meat, fresh or frozen

To prepare Hollandaise sauce, bring vinegar, water, peppercorns and bay leaf to a boil and reduce to about 2 tablespoons. Strain into a double boiler, cool slightly and stir in yolks. Keeping the double boiler over low heat, add butter in small cubes, one at a time, stirring constantly so that each piece is completely mixed before adding the next one. Sauce will gradually thicken. Season sauce and cover with waxed paper. Avoid overheating because hollandaise will curdle. Keep warm until needed.

Pan fry chicken breasts in a light vegetable oil. Blanch fresh asparagus in boiling water, then remove and set aside. To serve, place two asparagus spears on top of cooked chicken, top with crab meat and Hollandaise sauce. Place under a broiler to reheat slightly. Serves 6.

LINGUINI MARCO POLO
Café Chianti

Any ship's cook, able to prepare this succulent dish during one of Marco Polo's long sea voyages, would have been well rewarded by the master.

2 tablespoons butter
1 garlic clove, minced

2 tablespoons fresh parsley, chopped
    (1 teaspoon dried)
1 pound deboned chicken breast, cut in 1-inch
    squares
1 small red pepper, sliced 1 1/2-inch lengths
1 cup mushrooms, sliced
1 1/2 teaspoon fresh tarragon leaves, chopped
    (1/2 teaspoon dried)
pinch of pepper
1/4 teaspoon chicken bouillon powder (or
    to taste)
1/2 cup dry white wine
3/4 cup heavy cream (35% m.f.)
1 pound fresh linguini pasta
1/4 cup Parmesan cheese, grated

In a skillet melt butter over medium-high heat and sauté garlic. Add parsley and chicken slices and sauté until chicken is browned. With a slotted spoon remove chicken and keep warm. Add mushrooms, red pepper, tarragon, pepper and chicken bouillon to skillet and sauté until vegetables are tender-crisp. Remove vegetables with slotted spoon and reserve with the chicken.

Add wine to deglaze the pan; add cream and reduce until slightly thickened. Return chicken and vegetables to sauce. Meanwhile, prepare the linguini according to directions until *al dente*. Pour sauce over linguini and toss to mix. Serve on dinner plates garnished with fresh Parmesan. Serves 4.

ST. MARTINS STUFFED LEG OF LAMB
St. Martins Country Inn

Fresh spring lamb is always a treat, but this stuffed and rolled version makes an attractive dish for a special occasion. For ease of preparation, we suggest you ask your butcher to debone the leg.

1 leg of lamb (3-4 pounds), deboned
1/4 cup vegetable oil
1 small onion, diced
1/2 cup diced celery
5 to 6 cups soft breadcrumbs
1/2 teaspoon poultry seasoning
1 egg, beaten
1 teaspoon salt
Dash pepper and paprika
2 tablespoons flour
2 tablespoons vegetable oil (2nd amount)
1/2 cup boiling water
1/2 cup crabapple or red currant jelly
1/4 cup lemon juice
1 teaspoon grated lemon rind

Spread deboned lamb between two pieces of waxed paper and flatten to a uniform thickness with a meat mallet.

Heat first amount of oil (1/4 cup) and sauté onion and celery until tender. Set aside to cool slightly. Combine breadcrumbs, poultry seasoning, onion, celery and beaten egg and spread evenly over meat. Roll up jelly-roll fashion and tie tightly. Combine salt, pepper, paprika and flour on a large piece of waxed paper. Rub mixture over meat roll.

Heat second amount of oil (2 tablespoons) in a roasting pan; sear roll on all sides. Place a wire rack in bottom of roasting pan, add boiling water. Roast on rack in covered pan at 350°F 1 1/2 to 2 hours. Combine jelly, lemon juice and lemon rind. Spread over meat and continue baking, uncovered, for another 30 minutes, basting frequently. Serves 6.

LAMB SKEWERS WITH RED PEPPER AND ROSEMARY BUTTER
Café Chianti

This rendition of lamb kebabs drizzled in seasoned butter has a subtle Mediterranean flavour. Prepare everything in advance and when guests arrive merely turn on the grill; presto, you have an elegant entrée.

1 pound lamb, cut in 1 1/2-inch cubes
1/2 cup olive oil
1/4 cup fresh lemon juice
dash of salt and pepper
1 teaspoon dried oregano
1/2 red onion, quartered and segmented
cherry tomatoes
1/2 cup Red Pepper and Rosemary Butter

In a bowl, whisk together oil, lemon and seasonings. Marinate lamb in oil mixture for at least 2 hours. Toss vegetables in marinade just before assembling. Thread on skewer in this order; tomato, lamb, two layers of onion, lamb and repeat until skewer is filled. Grill on a hot barbecue until meat is cooked.

Serve with melted Red Pepper and Rosemary Butter (see below) and garnish with lemon slices and a sprig of fresh rosemary. Serves 4.

Red Pepper and Rosemary Butter
1 red pepper
1 cup butter
1 teaspoon fresh rosemary (1/2 teaspoon dried)

Grill pepper until it is burnt black on all sides. Immediately place in brown paper bag until cooled. Peel blackened skin from pepper. Remove stalk and inner seeds.

Combine pepper, butter and rosemary in a food processor and blend well. Reserve 1/2 cup for skewers and spoon out remaining butter in a tubelike fashion on cellowrap. Roll up and seal ends. This may be frozen and portions broken off and melted to serve with fish and other meats. Makes 1 cup.

St. Martins Country Inn

Glenora Inn and Distillery

SPRING LAMB CHOPS
Glenora Inn and Distillery

This simple version of grilled lamb chops will become a family favourite. Take care not to overcook the meat because lamb chops are small and will grill in a few minutes.

8 loin lamb chops (3 to 4 ounces each)
1/2 cup olive oil
1 tablespoon chokecherry vinegar or raspberry
    wine vinegar
fresh rosemary, to taste

Combine oil, vinegar and rosemary in a shallow dish. Place chops in marinade and turn to coat. Marinate 1 hour and then grill on a barbecue or broiler until meat is browned on the outside and pink on the inside. Serves 4.

RACK OF LAMB PROVENÇALE
Nemo's Restaurant

"French style" racks of lamb are available in the frozen foods section of most large supermarkets. At serving time, simply slice between the bones, allowing three or four ribs per serving.

2 racks of lamb, 12 to 14 ounces each
1 tablespoon vegetable oil
salt and pepper, to taste
1/4 cup Dijon mustard
1/3 cup dry breadcrumbs
1 1/2 teaspoons each dried thyme and
rosemary, crumbled
2 tablespoons soft butter

Demi-glace
1 package Knorr demi-glace
1 cup cold water
1/4 cup red wine
1 sprig fresh rosemary or 1 teaspoon dried,
tied in a piece of cheesecloth

Cabot Trail, Cape Breton, N.S.

Heat oil in roasting pan and quickly brown lamb racks on both sides. Remove from pan and season with salt and pepper.

Spread mustard over meaty side of lamb racks. In a mixing bowl combine crumbs, thyme, rosemary and butter. Dip lamb racks in crumbs to evenly coat mustard mixture. Bake in a preheated 400°F oven for 25 to 30 minutes for pink lamb, or until desired doneness.

While racks are baking prepare demi-glace by adding package contents and rosemary to water and wine in a small saucepan. Bring to a boil over medium-high heat, stirring frequently. Reduce heat and simmer to reduce slightly, about 10 minutes. Remove rosemary and keep warm.

After racks are cooked, cover and let stand 5 minutes on a cutting board, before serving.

To serve, slice lamb between the bones and set each serving in a pool of demi-glace with preferred choice of potatoes and vegetables. Serves 4.

BEEF TIPS MADAGASCAR
Campbell House

Mango chutney, Grand Marnier liqueur, honey and a hint of curry are expertly combined to make this beef dish a memorable feast. At Campbell House it is served on basmati rice.

1 1/2 pounds beef sirloin or tenderloin
1 tablespoon vegetable oil
2 teaspoons crushed green peppercorns
1/4 cup mango chutney
1/4 cup Grand Marnier liqueur
1/4 cup liquid honey
1/4 teaspoon Madras curry powder
1/4 cup orange marmalade
1/4 cup brandy

Slice beef in strips and brown in oil on medium high heat (add more oil if necessary). Remove meat from skillet and reserve. Combine remaining ingredients, place in skillet and cook over medium heat for 5 minutes. Add reserved beef and cook until sauce is thickened, approximately 10 minutes. Serves 4.

McCrady's Green Acres

PEPPERSTEAK WITH HOLLANDAISE
McCrady's Green Acres

Truly a peppersteak with a difference, this version is topped with a golden Hollandaise and a medley of colourful sweet peppers.

4 striploin steaks (6 ounces each)
2 tablespoons black peppercorns, crushed
1 tablespoon each red, green and yellow
    peppers, julienne strips
1 teaspoon green peppercorns
1 cup Hollandaise sauce (see page 71)

Coat steaks with crushed black peppercorns. Barbecue or broil to desired doneness. Meanwhile add peppers and green peppercorns to heated Hollandaise sauce. Serve steaks topped with sauce. Serves 4.

BEEF BOURGUIGNONNE
Steamers Stop Inn

Slow cooking is the key to this Beef Bourgignonne's flavour and tenderness. We suggest you use a good quality beef and a full bodied red wine.

1 1/2 pounds beef cubed
1/4 cup flour
2 tablespoons vegetable oil
2 tablespoon butter
1 large onion, chopped
1 clove garlic, crushed
3 tablespoons flour (2nd amount)
1 cup red wine
2 cups beef broth
1 tablespoon tomato paste
1 bay leaf
1 tablespoon each of fresh thyme, parsley and
    marjoram (or 1 teaspoon each dried)
20 mushroom caps
3 large carrots cut in 1-inch rounds
4 slices bacon, diced and fried
Salt and pepper, to taste

Cut and trim beef into cubes, dust with flour. In a heavy bottomed skillet, heat vegetable oil and sear beef cubes, a few at a time, turning often. Remove to a warm platter. Add butter to skillet. Sauté onion and garlic over medium heat until golden. Remove from heat and sprinkle with second amount of flour. Return to heat and slowly stir in wine, broth, tomato paste and seasonings. Thicken slightly over medium heat, add meat, vegetables and bacon. Season with salt and pepper, cover and simmer over low heat 1 hour or until meat is tender. Serves 4.

Wood Islands Ferry Lighthouse

PORK TENDERLOIN WITH PEPPERCORN-MUSTARD CRUST AND CIDER GRAVY
Auberge le Vieux Presbytère de Bouctouche 1880

Chef de cuisine Marcelle Albert carefully plans her menu at Le Tire-bouchon — "The Corkscrew" — diningroom. Her pork tenderloin with peppercorn mustard crust and cider gravy is a hallmark recipe.

2 pork tenderloins, about 1 1/2 pounds total
2 tablespoons butter
1 tablespoon flour
1 tablespoon Dijon mustard
1/2 tablespoon each cracked black, green and
    white peppercorns
1/2 tablespoon whole mustard seeds
1 teaspoon brown sugar
1 teaspoon dried thyme, crumbled

Cider Gravy
1 cup sweet apple cider
2 tablespoons Cognac
1 1/2 tablespoons flour
1/3 cup chicken broth or stock
2 teaspoons cider vinegar
2/3 teaspoon Dijon mustard
salt and pepper

Remove all fat and tissue from tenderloins and tuck tail under so meat is of uniform thickness. Combine butter, flour, mustard, cracked peppercorns, mustard seeds, brown sugar and thyme in a bowl. Spread paste over top and sides of tenderloins and bake in a preheated 350°F oven for 35 minutes until internal temperature reaches 165°F and meat is just barely pink inside. Transfer meat to a cutting board and tent with foil.

Place 1 1/2 tablespoons of pan drippings in a heavy saucepan and reserve. Discard remaining drippings from roasting pan and place pan over medium-low heat. Deglaze pan with cider. Boil until liquid is reduced by half, about 6 minutes; stir in Cognac and boil 1 minute longer.

Heat reserved drippings in saucepan over medium-high heat, add flour and stir until golden brown, about 2 minutes. Whisk in cider mixture from the roasting pan and stock. Simmer until thickened, stirring occasionally, about 2 minutes. Remove from heat and mix in vinegar and mustard. Season with salt and pepper.

Carve meat and serve with gravy. Serves 4.

PORK STROGANOFF
The Cobequid Inn

Nancy Cleveland tells us this dish freezes well but that the sour cream should be added after thawing. Double the recipe and you have dinner prepared for another day!

1/2 red pepper, thin julienne strips
1/2 green pepper, thin julienne strips
3 teaspoons vegetable oil
1 pound lean pork, thinly sliced
1 medium onion, chopped
1/2 lb. fresh mushrooms, halved
1 cup beef broth
1 tablespoon tomato paste
1 teaspoon Worcestershire sauce
1 teaspoon each, salt and pepper
2 tablespoons flour mixed in 3 tablespoons
    water
3 tablespoons dry sherry or 1/4 cup dark beer
1/3 cup light sour cream

Sauté pepper strips in 1 teaspoon of vegetable oil until crisp tender, 3 to 4 minutes. Reserve peppers and wipe out pan. Brown pork and onion in remaining oil. Add mushrooms and cook an additional two minutes.

 In a large kettle blend together broth, tomato paste, Worcestershire sauce, salt and pepper. Whisk in the flour mixture and bring to a boil, simmering until thickened. Add the meat mixture and simmer. Stir in peppers, sherry (or beer) and sour cream. Bring back to serving temperature, being careful not to boil. Serve over hot noodles. Serves 4.

VITELLO AL CONTIDINA
La Perla

La Perla in Dartmouth specializes in Northern Italian cuisine. Their scaloppini is one of the best veal offerings in the Maritimes.

1 1/2 pounds veal scallopini, trimmed
flour for dredging
olive oil
1/2 pound white mushrooms, sliced
1 can artichoke hearts, drained and cut into
    quarters
1/2 pound fresh asparagus, steamed
1/2 cup dry Marsala wine
1 cup heavy cream
salt and pepper to taste

Dredge veal in flour. Heat oil in a large skillet. Add veal and sauté approximately 30 seconds on each side. Remove to a warm plate. Drain any excess oil from the pan. Add mushrooms, artichokes, asparagus and veal to pan. Add Marsala and reduce volume by half. Add cream, salt and pepper. Reduce over medium heat until cream thickens slightly, about 5 minutes. Serves 4 to 6.

The Cobequid Inn

Grain silos, Shubenacadie

ROASTED PORK LOIN WITH PRUNE AND APPLE
Gowrie House Country Inn

Clifford Matthews of Gowrie House Country Inn has the ability to find and create wonderful recipes. Save this one for a special occasion — a time when you want to impress your guests.

1 tablespoon salt
1/2 teaspoon each of allspice, ground bay
    leaves and thyme
3 to 4 pounds pork loin, deboned and tied
1/4 cup olive oil
16 pitted prunes
1 cup chicken stock
1/2 cup dry white wine
2 or 3 Granny Smith apples
1/2 cup sugar
1/2 teaspoon allspice (2nd amount)
2 tablespoons butter, melted

Mix together salt, allspice, bay and thyme. Rub pork with olive oil and spices. Place in a plastic bag and refrigerate for several hours. Before preparing loin for roasting, remove it from the refrigerator and allow it to come to room temperature.

Meanwhile, prepare prune and apple garnish. Add prunes, stock and wine to a saucepan and simmer until prunes are plumped. Strain and reserve the prune juice. Peel, core and section the apples into eighths. Combine sugar and allspice and coat the apple segments. Place apples in a baking dish and drizzle with melted butter. Reserve to cook with loin.

Preheat oven to broil. Place meat in a broiler pan and cook 4 inches from heat for 12 to 14 minutes on each side. Reduce heat to 350°F. Place pork loin and dish of apples on center rack of oven and bake 25 to 30 minutes, until the internal temperature of the meat reaches 150°F and the apples are browned and soft. Reserve meat on a warm platter, cover lightly with foil.

Add the reserved prune liquid to the pan juices, and deglaze the pan over medium-high heat. Warm the prunes in a microwave oven, approximately 1 minute on high.

To serve, thinly slice pork, garnish with prunes and apple segments and drizzle pan juices over all. Serves 6.

Gnocchi Verdi (La Perla)

GNOCCHI VERDI
La Perla

This Italian delight is often served in place of potatoes or as a garnish to soups. Served with a side salad, Gnocchi Verdi makes a nutritious vegetarian meal.

4 tablespoons butter
1 1/2 pounds spinach, washed, deveined and
    chopped fine
3/4 cup ricotta cheese
2 eggs lightly beaten
6 tablespoons flour
3/4 cup freshly grated Parmesan cheese
1/2 teaspoon salt
1/2 teaspoon freshly ground black pepper
pinch of nutmeg
1 tablespoon butter, melted

Melt 4 tablespoons of butter in a large skillet and sauté prepared spinach until all the moisture has boiled away and spinach begins to stick to the pan. Add the ricotta and cook, stirring frequently, for a few minutes.

Transfer spinach mixture to a bowl and mix in eggs, flour, 1/4 cup of the Parmesan cheese, salt, pepper and nutmeg. Refrigerate for 30 minutes to 1 hour or until mixture is firm.

Fill a large pot with salted water, bring to a boil and reduce to simmer. Shape the dough into small balls, drop into water and boil until slightly firm to touch, about 7 minutes.

Butter a baking dish and place gnocchi in a single layer, pour over a little melted butter and remaining Parmesan cheese. Broil until the cheese browns. Serves 6.

HUGUENOT SPINACH GNOCCHI WITH COULIS DE TOMATES
Chez La Vigne

We have included two separate gnocchi recipes because of their variation. Alex Clavel's Huguenot styled gnocchi with a tomato sauce is a full course in itself and a most tempting one at that.

3/4 cup all purpose flour
1 pinch each of salt, pepper and grated nutmeg
2 eggs, slightly beaten
1/2 cup milk
1/3 cup water
6 tablespoons unsalted butter
1 3/4 cups fresh breadcrumbs
2 tablespoons fresh parsley, finely chopped
2 tablespoons fresh chives, finely chopped
1/4 pound fresh spinach, cooked, well drained
    and finely chopped
1/2 cup freshly grated Parmesan cheese

In a bowl combine flour and salt, pepper and nutmeg. Quickly whisk egg, milk and water into flour to make a light dough. In a skillet, over low heat, melt 3 tablespoons of the butter, add the breadcrumbs and stir and cook until the crumbs are golden brown. Add parsley, chives and spinach to the crumbs combining well.

Mix the crumbs into the dough and set aside to rest for one hour.

Meanwhile, heat a large pot of boiling salted water. Using two tablespoons, shape the dough into balls and drop into the boiling water. When cooked, approximately 7 minutes, the gnocchi will rise to the top of the water. Remove with a slotted spoon and place in a single layer in a buttered casserole. Sprinkle gnocchi with Parmesan and the remaining 3 tablespoons of butter which has been heated and cooked to a brown stage. Bake in a preheated 400°F oven, approximately 5 to 7 minutes, until bubbly. Serve topped with Coulis de tomates. Serves 4.

Coulis de tomates
3 tablespoons heavy cream (35% m.f.)
1/2 small leek, white part cut in fine strips
1/2 onion, finely chopped
1 garlic clove, finely chopped
3 fresh basil leaves, chopped

1/2 pound ripe tomatoes, peeled, juice
    squeezed out and diced
salt to taste

In a small saucepan, place cream, leek, onion and basil. Cover and simmer for 10 minutes at medium heat. Add tomatoes and cook additional 5 minutes. Purée the mixture in a food processor. Add salt to taste. Pour coulis over gnocchi to serve.

The Lookoff, Annapolis Valley

MANICOTTI CRÊPES
Acton's Grill and Cafe

Chef Werner says, "This is best eaten with fresh garden greens tossed with a vinaigrette." We followed his advice and our family raved over the result.

12 savory crêpes
1/2 pound ricotta cheese
1 cup mozzarella cheese, grated
1/2 cup Parmesan cheese, grated
2 tablespoons fresh herbs, chopped
(combination of basil, oregano, parsley and thyme) or 1 1/4 teaspoon dried combination
2 eggs
dash salt & pepper
3 cups tomato sauce (see page 7)

Prepare savory crêpes (see below) and set aside to cool. Combine remaining ingredients (except tomatoe sauce), blending well and chill for 1 hour.

To assemble, spread approximately 2 tablespoons of cheese filling lengthwise on each crêpe and roll up. Place crêpes, side-by-side, in a greased, ovenproof baking dish. Cover with tomato sauce and a sprinkling of Parmesan cheese.

Bake in 400°F oven for 15 to 20 minutes until manicotti has lightly "puffed". Remove from oven and let rest for 10 minutes before serving. Serves 6.

Savory Crêpes
2 eggs
1 cup milk
3/4 cup flour
2 tablespoons fresh parsley, chopped (1 1/2 teaspoon dried)
pinch of salt

Whisk together eggs and milk. Add flour and seasonings and continue beating until the batter is smooth. Rest batter for 1 hour.

Brush a non-stick skillet with a little vegetable oil and bring to a medium heat. Add enough batter to barely cover the bottom of the pan (1/4 cup) and cook for approximately 30 seconds. Flip crêpe and cook another 15 seconds. Repeat, setting crêpes aside to cool. Makes approximately 1 dozen crêpes.

Acton's Grill and Café

Pesto Stuffed Tomatoes (MacAskill's Restaurant)

VEGETABLES

Vegetables are an important part of meal planning and while gathering recipes for this book we often asked the chefs to suggest vegetables to accompany their dishes. Invariably, when asked to describe how they prepare each dish, they would humbly reply, "Oh, it's nothing. I just stir fry a little of this or add a little of that." The result at the restaurant is a mouth watering treat and we felt we wanted to offer recipes that even a novice cook would feel confident to try. In the end, we managed to convince a few chefs to share their vegetable recipes with us and the results are exciting!

First and foremost, it is not necessary to cook vegetables to a soggy death. Most early summer varieties are best served "crisp tender" and we suggest you try the *Vegetable Stir Fry* from Shaw's Hotel which is flavoured with a hint of sesame oil or *Grilled Vegetables* from Cooper's Inn which take on the sweet taste of rosemary and thyme while they marinate in a gentle olive oil and vermouth marinade. Both recipes are quick to prepare, appealing to the eye and very tasty.

Several recipes featured adapt well to serving from a buffet table. Look for dishes that can be prepared in an oven-to-table casserole, such as Normaway's *Vegetable Moussaka* or the delicious *Braised Cabbage* from Marshlands Inn.

Potatoes are major agricultural crops in New Brunswick and Prince Edward Island and we decided it was fitting to include a few recipes that would highlight their versatility. *Cheese Potatoes* from the Walker Inn or *Tatties and Neeps*, the old fashioned speciality from the Duncreigan Country Inn, are but two wonderful examples of this tasty inexpensive vegetable.

Choose your vegetable dishes to complement your main course. Root vegetables such as turnip and winter squash go well with roasts, while seafoods require delicately flavoured vegetables, such as fresh green beans or zucchini. Be daring and experiment by substituting some of the vegetables suggested in these recipes. We are sure you will enjoy the results.

PESTO STUFFED TOMATOES
MacAskill's Restaurant

We tested this recipe in the height of summer when the tomatoes were vine ripe and the basil was fresh in the garden. The result was aromatic and filled with summer tastes. Substitute specialty store pesto in winter, if fresh basil is not available, and you will come close to recapturing the summer.

1 cup lightly packed fresh basil
2 cloves garlic
2 teaspoons pine nuts
1/4 cup Parmesan cheese
1 tablespoon olive oil
dash of salt
grating of fresh pepper
3 small to medium tomatoes

To make pesto combine basil, garlic, pine nuts, 1 tablespoon of Parmesan cheese, olive oil, salt and pepper in a food processor and process until smooth. Reserve.

Slice off ends of tomatoes. Insert paring knife at the 'equator' of the tomato and cut in a zig-zag pattern around the circumference. Gently pull the two halves of the tomato apart and using a teaspoon, delicately remove the seeds and insides. Evenly divide the pesto among the tomato crowns and top with remaining Parmesan cheese. Bake in a preheated 350°F oven for 7 to 10 minutes, until cheese is browned. Serves 6.

CHEESE POTATOES
The Walker Inn

This easy to prepare dish offers a nice change from the traditional methods of cooking potatoes. The vegetables may be prepared in advance and assembled just before cooking.

4 large potatoes, cooked whole
mozzarella cheese slices
1/2 teaspoon each of paprika, garlic salt, parsley flakes

Peel and slice potatoes. In a lightly greased shallow casserole, arrange potatoes so that the slices are overlapping. Top potatoes with thin slices of mozzarella. Combine herbs and sprinkle over cheese. Bake in a preheated 350°F oven until the cheese is melted, approximately 7 to 10 minutes. Serves 4 to 6.

Chez Françoise

DUCHESS POTATOES
Chez Françoise

At Chez Françoise this dish is prepared in the classic manner. It is an excellent accompaniment to scallops or tenderloins.

4 potatoes, scrubbed (1 1/2 pounds)
2 egg yolks, beaten
1 tablespoon blend (10% m.f.)
1/4 cup Parmesan cheese
2 tablespoons butter
salt and white ground pepper, to taste
dash paprika

Boil potatoes in a large saucepan in salted water. Drain and return pot to the stove for a couple of minutes to dry the outside of the potatoes. Cool slightly and peel.
   Press potatoes through a potato ricer or sieve and return to pan. Mix in egg yolks, blend, cheese and butter, and beat until potatoes are light and fluffy. Season with salt and pepper and spoon mixture into a pastry bag. Pipe potatoes onto a buttered baking dish. Sprinkle with paprika and broil, 6 inches from heat until brown. Serves 4.

ROSEMARY LYONNAISE POTATOES
Duncreigan Country Inn of Mabou

There is nothing to compare with the taste of tiny new potatoes. Sautéed in garlic and olive oil with a hint of rosemary, they make a wonderful side dish for meats and seafood. We especially enjoyed this dish served with roast lamb.

1 1/4 pounds small, new red potatoes
2 tablespoons olive oil
3/4 cup onion, finely chopped
1 clove garlic, minced
1 tablespoon fresh rosemary, chopped
    (1 teaspoon dried, crushed)
salt and pepper to taste

Clean, but do not peel potatoes. Boil them in salted water until almost cooked; drain well. In a large skillet heat oil and sauté onion, garlic and rosemary until onion is softened. Add cooked potatoes to skillet and lightly brown. Serves 6.

Covered bridge near Sussex, N.B.

DELI CARROTS
Quaco Inn

At the Quaco Inn, Marilyn Landry serves this dish as a warm vegetable with several of her entrées. We also tested it with less sugar and served it cold as a salad, with excellent results.

3 pounds carrots, pared and cut on the bias
1 can tomato soup
1/2 cup vinegar
1 scant cup sugar
1 tablespoon Dijon style mustard
1 teaspoon Worcestershire sauce
1/2 each red and green pepper, thinly sliced
1 small onion, thinly sliced

Boil carrots in a small amount of salted water, only until crisp.

Whisk together tomato soup, vinegar, sugar, mustard and Worcestershire sauce. Add peppers and onion. Pour sauce over carrots and serve either warm or cold. Serves 6-8.

TATTIES AND NEEPS (POTATOES AND TURNIPS)
Duncreigan Country Inn of Mabou

Tatties and Neeps are a wonderful addition to a roast or meat dish. They can be prepared early in the day and reheated at serving time. Variations of this traditional Mabou recipe include using carrots in place of turnips or adding cheese to the neeps.

1 small turnip, peeled and cubed
1 medium onion, diced
4 large potatoes, peeled and quartered
1/4 cup butter
salt and pepper, to taste

Boil turnip and onion in a small saucepan until tender. Drain, reserving cooking liquid. Boil potatoes in a separate saucepan until tender. Drain, then dry potatoes over low heat, breaking up with a fork to allow steam to escape. Mash potatoes and gradually add butter and 1 teaspoon of cooking water to make a stiff mashed potato. Season with salt and pepper and cool slightly.

Quaco Inn

Place reserved turnip and onion in a food processor and purée. Blend into potatoes and place in a piping bag with a large star tip. Pipe onto a cookie sheet that has been lined with greased waxed paper. Chill uncovered, until firm.

To serve, place on a cookie sheet and reheat at 350°F for about 20 minutes. Serves 6 to 8.

GRILLED VEGETABLES
Cooper's Inn and Restaurant

We found this vegetable recipe to be one of the easiest and tastiest in our book. You are not limited to the vegetables listed in our ingredients and may substitute any seasonal fare that grills well.

4 to 6 cups of summer vegetables, cut in
    portions suitable for grilling (zucchini,
    pattypan squash cubes, sweet pepper
    squares, whole mushrooms etc.)
1/3 cup olive oil
3 tablespoons lemon juice
3 tablespoons dry white vermouth
1 tablespoon ground rosemary
1 1/2 teaspoon dried thyme
1/4 teaspoon salt
1/4 teaspoon sugar
freshly ground pepper

Prepare vegetables. In a bowl whisk together remaining ingredients until well combined. Marinate vegetables in oil mixture for at least 30 minutes. Heat a grill or barbecue and place in a grilling basket and cook for 5 minutes on each side until browned and cooked through.

Marinade is sufficient for 4 to 6 cups of prepared vegetables. Allow 1 cup of prepared vegetables per serving. Serves 4 to 6.

Shaw's Hotel

VEGETABLE MEDLEY STIR FRY
Shaw's Hotel

A hint of sesame turns this vegetable medley into a gourmet's delight! Experiment with different vegetables, but be sure that they require about the same cooking time.

1 tablespoon vegetable oil
1 medium onion, cut in wedges
1 clove garlic, minced
1 cup broccoli flowerets
1 cup cauliflower flowerets
1 small zucchini, sliced
1 tablespoon soya sauce

1 teaspoon lemon pepper*
1/2 teaspoon sesame oil
2 small tomatoes, cut in wedges
1 tablespoon sesame seeds, toasted

Heat oil in a wok or large skillet over medium heat. Add onion and garlic, stir fry until onion starts to soften. Add broccoli and cauliflower and stir fry about 2 minutes. Add zucchini and cook an additional 2 minutes, until crisp tender. Stir in soya sauce, lemon pepper and sesame oil. Add tomato wedges and cook one minute. Sprinkle with toasted sesame seeds. Serves 4 to 6.

* sold in specialty food stores

The Normaway Inn

VEGETABLE MOUSSAKA
The Normaway Inn

This recipe may take a little longer to prepare but the time is well worth the effort. With its aromatic Mediterranean flavour we found it a delicious accompaniment for grilled seafood and meats. You might want to garnish Vegetable Moussaka with black olives and serve with hot garlic bread to make an ample luncheon dish.

1 medium eggplant
1 1/2 tablespoons coarse salt
1/4 cup olive oil
2 8-inch zucchinis
1 cup ricotta or cottage cheese
1/2 cup Parmesan cheese
3 eggs, lightly beaten
1/2 cup heavy cream (35% m.f.)
1/2 teaspoon dried oregano
dash of salt and pepper
1/2 cup peeled, chopped tomatoes
2 large or 3 medium tomatoes, sliced

Cut eggplant into slices 1/3-inch thick. Sprinkle with salt and layer in a colander. Place a heavy weight on top and let stand for 2 hours to let the bitterness drain out. Rinse well under cold water and then dry, squeezing out excess water with paper towels. Brush slices with olive oil and bake in a preheated 350°F oven, turning once, until golden, approximately 20 minutes. Reserve.

Slice zucchini on a bias, 1/4-inch thick. Brush with olive oil and bake in a preheated 425°F oven, turning once, until golden, approximately 5 minutes. Reserve.

In a bowl combine cheeses, eggs, cream and seasonings and blend well.

To assemble moussaka, lightly grease an 8-cup casserole dish and place chopped tomatoes in bottom. Arrange a layer each of eggplant, zucchini and sliced tomatoes. Repeat with three more layers. Pour egg mixture over vegetables shaking casserole to distribute custard through layers. Bake in a preheated 325°F oven for 1 hour or until set and golden. Remove from oven and rest for 10 minutes.

Serve as a vegetable with meat or seafood entrées or as an appetizer on tomato sauce garnished with black olives. Serves 4 to 6 as an appetizer or 8 generously as a vegetable.

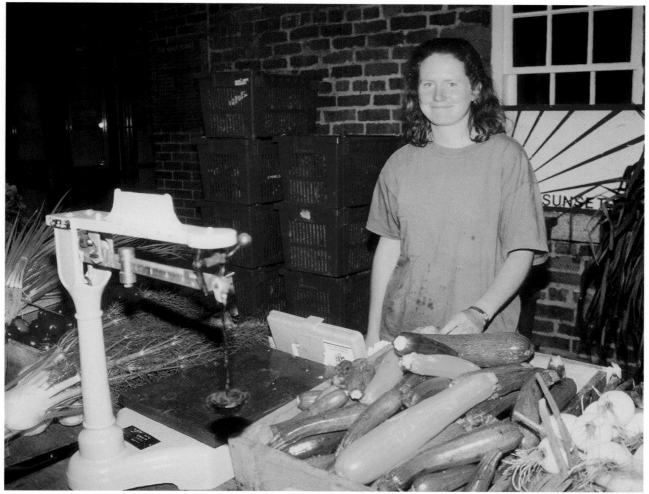

Halifax Farmers' Market

ZUCCHINI BASIL PANCAKES
Duncreigan Country Inn of Mabou

Eleanor Mullendore of Duncreigan Country Inn says that this is a good use for all those surplus zucchini at the end of the summer!

3 cups grated zucchini
salt to season
1 egg
1/4 cup milk
1/4 teaspoon hot sauce (e.g. Tabasco)
freshly ground pepper, to taste
2 tablespoons basil and/or parsley, finely chopped
1/2 cup flour
1/4 cup grated Parmesan cheese
1 1/2 teaspoons baking powder

Peel, remove seeds and grate zucchini. Lightly salt the zucchini and place in a colander covered with a weighted plate; let stand 30 minutes and then squeeze out excess liquid.

In a bowl, beat together, egg, milk, hot sauce, pepper to taste and herbs. Add zucchini to egg mixture, stirring to combine. Mix together flour, cheese and baking powder and add to the egg mixture, stirring well. Preheat a greased skillet to 400°F. Spoon 3 to 4 tablespoons of batter on skillet and cook about 3 minutes on one side, until brown; flip and cook 1 minute more. Top with butter as and serve as a side dish for entrées. Serves 6.

Marshlands Inn

VEGETARIAN ZUCCHINI BAKE
Salmon River House Country Inn

This is a great dish to prepare when zucchini and tomatoes are overflowing in your garden. Tasty and flavourful, it is a good choice to accompany meat and seafood.

4 small or 3 medium-sized zucchinis
2 tablespoons butter
1 garlic clove, crushed
1 small onion, diced
4 medium tomatoes, diced 1/4-inch cubes
1 teaspoon each of sweet basil and oregano
salt and pepper to taste
1/4 cup grated Parmesan cheese
1/2 cup mozzarella cheese, grated
buttered breadcrumbs

Slice the zucchini on the bias into 1/4-inch slices. In a skillet, melt butter. Add garlic, then zucchini and sauté until it is browned and slightly transparent. Remove zucchini and reserve. Add onion, tomatoes and seasoning to skillet and sauté for a few minutes until vegetables are softened.

Grease 4 oven-proof au-gratin dishes or an 8-cup casserole and layer zucchini, a sprinkling of Parmesan, a layer of tomatoes and another sprinkling of Parmesan. Repeat layers, ending with tomatoes and Parmesan. Cover layers with grated mozzarella and breadcrumbs. Bake in a preheated 350°F oven for 30 minutes until golden and bubbly. Serves 4.

BRAISED RED CABBAGE
Marshlands Inn

A hearty, flavourful dish, Marshlands' Braised Red Cabbage is delicious with pork and an innovative addition to a buffet table.

1/2 cup white vinegar
1/3 cup sugar
3/4 teaspoon nutmeg
2 apples, diced
red cabbage, shredded (about 1 1/4 pounds)

In a saucepan whisk together vinegar, sugar and nutmeg and cook over medium high heat until sugar is dissolved. Add apple and cabbage and simmer, covered, for 45 minutes. Drain excess liquid. Serves 6.

HARVARD BEETS
Marshlands Inn

While freshly cooked beets are preferred, this recipe transforms canned beets into a colorful and flavourful dish suitable for Guests.

2 cups sliced cooked beets (19-ounce can sliced
    beets)
1/4 cup cooking liquid
1/4 cup vinegar
4 teaspoons cornstarch
1 tablespoon vegetable oil
1/2 cup sugar

Combine beet liquid, vinegar, cornstarch, oil and sugar. Bring to a boil stirring frequently. Add beets to sauce and return to serving temperature. Serves 4.

TOMATO CHUTNEY
Liscombe Lodge

The inclusion of maple syrup in this chutney recipe gives it a unique sweet, yet tart, flavour. This condiment's great taste and pretty colour makes it a fitting addition to seafood, poultry and pork dishes.

2 1/2 pounds ripe, tomatoes, peeled and diced

Partridge berries

2 pounds tart apples, peeled, cored and sliced
1 1/4 cups sugar
3/4 cup maple syrup
2/3 cup cider vinegar
1 teaspoon mixed pickling spices
1/2 teaspoon whole cloves

Place tomatoes in a bowl, cover and put a heavy weight on top. Press overnight and in the morning, pour off juice. Transfer tomatoes to a large saucepan and add apples, sugar, maple syrup and vinegar. Tie up spices in a cheesecloth bag and add to the saucepan. Bring to a boil and simmer until thick, about 1 1/2 hours. Remove the spice bag. Pour chutney into hot sterilized jars and seal. Yields approximately 6 cups.

Banana Royale (The Galley)

DESSERTS

The dilemma of desserts! In this day and age when we are constantly warned to control our calorie and fat intake, and told to be more physically active in our drive to perfect ourselves, how can we possibly dive into a rich dessert with any conscience at all. We certainly don't want to become sweet sneaks scurrying off to a dark closet to eat creamy éclairs, nor do we want to become cynics who ridicule and scorn the enjoyment of food.

The only solution we arrived at, while still including a dessert section in our book, was to cry out "Moderation!" Life in moderation seems to be the most reasonable route to follow. With this in mind, we went in search of delectable desserts from the chefs of our Maritime restaurants asking them to share a sampling of decadent, semi-decadent and downright healthy recipes. They did not disappoint us.

As dessert is the finale to dinner, it should be in harmony with other courses of the meal, drawing it to a comfortable close. If you have served a rich main course, you may want to serve a light dessert, or conversely, if your entrée had little protein, a dessert made with milk or cheese will compliment the meal.

Summer dining begs for cool desserts and those that feature the bounty of our orchards and gardens. We recommend the fruit pie recipes or parfait-style dishes included in our desserts. During the cold days of winter, hot and hearty meals are in order and lend themselves to steamy puddings and warm cakes.

Be adventuresome and prepare some of these delicious desserts. Decide to go healthy or completely decadent — the choice is yours. Enjoy!

Salmon River House Country Inn

BANANA ROYALE
The Galley

We like to serve desserts that can be prepared in advance, leaving the hostess time to enjoy her guests. This recipe fills the bill.

3 tablespoons sugar (for syrup)
1/3 cup water
dark rum
2 tablespoons butter
1/2 cup brown sugar
1/4 teaspoon cinnamon
1/4 teaspoon nutmeg
1/4 cup blend
3 bananas, sliced
vanilla ice cream
whipped cream and fresh mint leaves to
    garnish, if desired

For rum syrup, combine 3 tablespoons sugar and water in a small saucepan and bring to a boil. Cook until sugar is dissolved and set aside to cool. Add an equal amount of dark rum to syrup and refrigerate.

For sauce, melt butter in a saucepan and stir in sugar, cinnamon, nutmeg, and blend. Whisk sauce and simmer until slightly thickened, about 5 minutes. Cool and store.

Before serving, heat butter sauce with sliced bananas. Place a scoop of ice cream in six serving dishes, top with banana sauce mixture and 2 tablespoons of rum syrup. Decorate with whipped cream and fresh mint leaves, if desired. Serves 6.

Ross Farm Museum, near Campbell House

FRESH FRUIT YOGHURT PARFAIT
Salmon River House Country Inn

Don't save this simple creation for dessert only. It is an excellent early morning starter or refreshing lunchtime meal.

2 to 3 cups fresh fruit of choice (orange,
    peach, pineapple, strawberry, raspberry etc.)
lemon juice
2 cups low-fat vanilla or natural yoghurt

Prepare fruit and chop. You may use one, two or several different kinds of fruit, depending on what is in season. Sprinkle with lemon juice to preserve colour. In a tall parfait or wine glass, place a spoonful of yoghurt followed by a spoonful of fruit. Alternate fruit and yoghurt to fill the glass; finish with yoghurt and top with a fresh berry or maraschino cherry. Serves 4.

CREAM CROWDIE
Campbell House

In Cream Crowdie, rolled oats and Drambuie reflect the strength of Scottish influence in Nova Scotian cooking.

3 tablespoons oatmeal
1 cup heavy cream (35% m.f.)
1 ounce Drambuie liqueur
1 tablespoon sugar
vanilla ice cream

Spread oatmeal evenly on a baking sheet and bake at 350°F for 10 minutes, until golden brown. Remove from oven and cool. Place cream in a chilled bowl and whip until stiff. Add cooled oatmeal, Drambuie and sugar. Place ice cream in a champagne glass, top with oatmeal-cream mixture. Serves 4 to 6.

Dutch Appel Taart (The Blomidon Inn)

DUTCH APPEL TAART
The Blomidon Inn

At the Blomidon Inn, only Annapolis Valley Red Delicious apples are used for this wonderful tart. We're sure that you won't compromise the results if you choose another variety of apple, but don't alter the sugar or the spices. They serve it garnished with whipped cream and toasted almond slices.

1 cup butter
2 cups flour
1 cup sugar
1 teaspoon baking powder
1 large egg, beaten
3 pounds Red Delicious apples, peeled and cored and diced in 1/4-inch pieces
1 tablespoon lemon juice
1 cup sugar
2 teaspoons nutmeg
2 tablespoons cinnamon
Pinch of cloves
3 tablespoons sherry

In a large mixing bowl, cut together butter, flour, sugar and baking powder. Incorporate beaten egg. While this crust mixture is still coarse and crumbly, reserve 1/2 cup for topping. Mix remainder into a ball press gently over the bottom and half way up the side of a greased and floured 10-inch springform pan. The dough should be of uniform thickness, just over 1/4 inch.

Mix together the prepared apples, lemon juice, sugar, spices and flavouring and place on the crust. The level of filling will exceed the height of the crust, but baking will compensate. Sprinkle with reserved topping and bake on the middle rack in a preheated oven at 375°F until top is a rich golden brown, approximately 1 hour. After baking, allow the *taart* to cool and then refrigerate. Unmold from springform pan and divide into 12 servings.

APPLE PIE
The Manor Inn

An apple pie to make Mum proud! We tested the Manor Inn's version with early Gravenstein apples with excellent results.

Pastry
1 3/4 cups flour
3/4 teaspoon salt
3/4 cup lard or shortening
4 - 5 tablespoons cold water

Combine flour and salt in a mixing bowl. Cut in shortening or lard with a pastry blender until mixture is the size of large peas. Sprinkle water on the dough, a little at a time, and blend it in lightly. Form the dough into a ball, handling it as little as possible.

Use a lightly floured surface, preferably with a pastry cloth and a covered rolling pin. Divide pastry into two and form each half into a flattened ball. Roll lightly from the centre until the pastry is about 1 inch larger than pie plate.

Roll pastry over rolling pin and transfer to a greased pie plate. Unroll and ease into place, being careful not to stretch the pastry. Trim off any excess.

Filling
4 cups peeled, cored and sliced apples
1 cup sugar
1/4 cup flour
1 teaspoon cinnamon
1/2 teaspoon nutmeg

Toss all ingredients together in a bowl. Place in unbaked pie shell. Cover with top crust and bake at 375°F for 35 to 40 minutes, until browned. Cool on a rack and refrigerate until ready to serve. Serves 6 to 8.

BLUEBERRY LEMON PIE
The Compass Rose, N.B.

Put this recipe in your file of "special occasion" desserts. The blueberry-lemon combination is delightful and the pie can be made any time using frozen berries.

1 large pie shell, prebaked and cooled
3 egg yolks
1 can Eagle Brand sweetened condensed milk
1/2 cup lemon juice
1 tablespoon lemon zest
4 cups blueberries
1/2 cup liquid honey
1/2 cup water
2 tablespoons cornstarch
2 teaspoons lemon juice
1 cup heavy cream (35% m.f.)
1/4 teaspoon almond extract
2 tablespoons liquid honey
1/4 cup toasted almond slivers

In a medium-sized bowl, beat together egg yolks, sweetened condensed milk, lemon juice and lemon zest. Pour into prepared pie crust and bake in a 350°F oven for 10 minutes. Remove from oven and let cool.

In a saucepan, combine 1 cup of blueberries, honey, water and cornstarch. Bring to boiling point and let simmer until thickened. Remove from heat and stir in lemon juice. Cool thoroughly and stir in 3 cups of blueberries. Spoon into pie shell over lemon mixture and refrigerate.

At serving time, whip cream, sweeten with honey and add almond flavoring. Spoon onto pie and sprinkle with almonds. Serves 6 to 8.

Blueberry picking

RASPBERRY PIE
Drury Lane Steak House

The addition of orange juice gives a touch of tartness to this fruit pie. At Drury Lane it is served with a dollop of whipping cream!

Pastry to make one 9-inch double crust pie
   (see page 102)
5 cups raspberries, fresh or frozen
1 tablespoon orange juice
1 cup sugar
1/3 cup flour
1/2 teaspoon salt

Mix together raspberries, orange juice, sugar, flour and salt. Line a pie plate with pastry, fill with berry mixture and cover with second piece of pastry. Flute edges, sprinkle crust with water and shake a small amount of sugar over the pie. Bake in a preheated 400°F oven 40 to 50 minutes. Serves 6 to 8.

BUMBLE BERRY PIE
Inverary Inn Resort

The chef at the Inverary Inn tells us that you can use any combination of fruit in Bumble Berry Pie, but you may have to adjust the sugar.

1/2 cup blueberries
1/2 cup strawberries, quartered
1/2 cup raspberries
1/2 cup blackberries
1/2 cup apples, finely sliced
1/2-3/4 cup sugar
1 tablespoon cornstarch
1/4 teaspoon cinnamon

Prepare a pastry of your choice to make a 9-inch pie. Mix together all ingredients and place in unbaked pie crust. Cover with pastry and bake at 350°F until golden brown, approximately 40 to 45 minutes.

RUM RUNNER PIE
The Matthew House Inn

Stories of the prohibition era and bootlegging on the Island abound, embellished, it seems, with every passing year! This recipe works best with a crumb crust, although a baked crust can be used. Prepare the crust ahead and chill it while making the filling.

Crust
2/3 cup graham cracker crumbs
2/3 cup finely ground hazelnuts
3 tablespoons sugar
1/3 cup butter, melted

Filling
1/3 cup cold water
1 envelope unflavored gelatin
2/3 cup sugar
4 egg yolks
1/4 cup dark rum (not spiced)
1 cup heavy cream (35% m.f.)

Garnish
1/3 cup heavy cream, whipped
Fresh fruit such as raspberries, strawberries
   or kiwi
Reserved hazelnuts

To prepare crust, combine dry ingredients, reserving 1 tablespoon of hazelnuts for garnish. Mix in butter, tossing to coat. Press over the bottom and up the sides of a 9-inch pie plate and bake at 350°F for 8 to 9 minutes. Cool, then chill.

For the filling, add gelatin to cold water in a small saucepan. Stir constantly over low heat, then medium heat to dissolve. In a separate bowl, beat sugar and egg yolks. Stir in hot gelatin. Slowly add rum, beating constantly.

In a chilled bowl, whip the cream into stiff peaks and then fold into the gelatin mixture. Set the bowl into a basin of crushed ice and whip until thick and starting to set, 7 to 10 minutes. Scoop into chilled pie shell. Cover with plastic wrap and chill 6 hours or overnight.

Garnish with freshly whipped cream and fresh fruit. Sprinkle with finely chopped hazelnuts.

At the Matthew House, this dessert is served with espresso. Serves 6.

BUTTERSCOTCH PIE
Steamers Stop Inn

This recipe makes a large, tall butterscotch pie. We are sure it will become a family favourite.

4 cups milk
2 cups brown sugar
1/4 cup butter
1/2 cup cornstarch
pinch of salt
2 eggs
1 teaspoon vanilla
1 deep 9-inch pie shell, baked and cooled
1 cup heavy cream (35% m.f.)

In a large saucepan over medium heat, bring 4 cups of milk, brown sugar and butter to a boil, stirring constantly.

In a bowl combine cornstarch, salt, 1/2 cup of the hot milk and eggs. Stir into hot milk mixture. Simmer until thickened. Remove from heat and stir in vanilla. Pour into pie shell. Chill. Serve with whipped cream. Yields 6 to 8 servings.

Saint John River near Gagetown, N.B.

Lemon Almond Tart (Acton's Grill and Café)

LEMON ALMOND TART
Acton's Grill and Café

We found the sharp lemon flavour of this tart a nice alternative to the sweetness of most desserts.

1 cup flour
3 1/2 tablespoons sugar
1/3 cup butter, softened
4 eggs
1/2 cup sugar (2nd amount)
zest of 1 1/2 lemons (thinly shaved rind)
1/2 cup lemon juice
3/4 cup almonds, finely ground
1/3 cup melted butter, cooled but still liquid
toasted, sliced almonds for garnish.

Combine flour and 3 1/2 tablespoons of sugar, mixing well. Add softened butter and combine until crumbly. Beat 1 egg and mix well into the pastry. Form into a ball. Chill pastry for at least 30 minutes. Roll out to uniform thickness for a 9-inch tart baking form. Weight down pastry shell or prick bottom of shell with a fork.

Partially cook the tart shell in a 375°F oven for 8 minutes. Meanwhile, with a whisk, beat together the remaining eggs, sugar, lemon rind, juice and almonds. Add melted butter and continue beating.

Pour the lemon mixture into the tart shell and bake at 375°F for an additional 25 to 30 minutes, until done. Remove from oven and allow the tart to cool. Garnish with toasted sliced almonds. Serves 8.

Rustico Bay, Prince Edward Island

COCONUT CREAM PIE
The West Point Lighthouse

This coconut cream pie recipe is for those who have difficulty making perfect meringue. Simply omit it and serve with a dollop of freshly whipped cream.

3/4 cup sugar
1/3 cup flour
2 tablespoons cornstarch
2 cups milk
2 eggs, beaten
1/2 cup sweetened coconut
baked pastry shell
1/2 cup heavy cream (35% m.f.)

In a large saucepan, combine sugar, flour and cornstarch. Gradually stir in milk. Bring mixture to a boil, stirring constantly, until it thickens. Cook over medium heat 2 minutes longer, then remove from heat. Stir small amount of hot mixture into eggs, return to hot mixture and cook two minutes, stirring constantly. Remove from heat and stir in coconut. Pour into a cooked prepared pie shell. Cool and top with whipped cream before serving. Serves 6 to 8.

PRIZE BUTTER TARTS
The West Point Lighthouse

These tasty little tarts store well and are delicious with a freshly brewed pot of tea.

1 cup brown sugar
1/3 cup butter, melted
1 teaspoon vanilla
1 egg, beaten
2 tablespoons milk
10 to 12 unbaked pastry tart shells

Mix together sugar, butter and vanilla. Stir in the egg and milk. Pour into prepared tart shells and bake 400°F for 15 minutes.

Picking strawberries

STRAWBERRIES IN PUFF PASTRY
The Loyalist Country Inn

What an impressive dessert to serve your favourite Valentine — or have your Valentine serve you!

6 to 8 puff pastry hearts or rounds (3 to 4
    inches each)
1 quart fresh strawberries, sliced. Reserve 12
    berries for garnish.
1 recipe Grand Marnier Pastry Cream

Prepare puff pastries from a 14-ounce package of frozen puff pastry, following package directions. Cool on a wire rack and split.
    Wash and slice berries, adding a small amount of sugar, if desired.

Pastry Cream
1 cup milk
2 egg yolks
1/4 cup sugar

2 tablespoons flour
1 1/2 tablespoons Grand Marnier
1 cup heavy cream, whipped
1 teaspoon icing sugar

Heat milk almost to boiling. In a bowl, beat egg yolks well with sugar; beat in flour. Slowly mix half the hot milk into the egg mixture, then gradually stir back into the remaining milk. Cook over low heat until the custard thickens and barely starts to boil. Remove from heat and cool over ice, stirring often. When completely cool stir in Grand Marnier. Whip cream and fold into milk-egg mixture. (Reserve a small amount of cream to use as a garnish).
    Split hearts and spoon pastry cream onto bottom halves. Place sliced berries on the cream. Place top half of hearts over berries and sprinkle remaining berries around hearts on plates. Dust pastries with icing sugar and garnish with whipped cream and fanned whole strawberries. Serves 6 to 8.

DOUBLE CHOCOLATE MARBLE CHEESECAKE
The Loyalist Country Inn

If you think all cheesecakes were created equal, try this treat from PEI's Loyalist Country Inn.

2 2/3 cups chocolate cookie crumbs
2/3 cup butter, melted
1 pound cream cheese, softened
1/2 cup sugar
1 cup heavy cream (35% m.f.)
1 1/2 package unflavoured gelatin softened in
    1/4 cup cold water
1/4 cup boiling water
1 ounce white crème de cacao
1 ounce brown crème de cacao
4 ounces white chocolate, melted and cooled
4 ounces milk chocolate, melted and cooled
1 cup heavy cream, whipped
Chocolate curls, or fresh berries and whipped
    cream for garnish

Combine chocolate cookie crumbs and melted butter and press into bottom and sides of 10-inch springform pan. Bake at 350°F for 10 minutes. Cool completely.

Beat cream cheese with sugar until light and fluffy. Add 1 cup of cream and continue beating.

Dissolve softened gelatin in 1/4 cup boiling water. Add gelatin to cheese mixture. Divide mixture in half. Add white crème de cacao and white chocolate to one half of mixture. Add brown crème de cacao and milk chocolate to remaining mixture. Divide whipped cream and fold half into each of the cheese mixtures. Swirl the two mixtures together over chocolate crumb crust, in springform pan. Chill 4 hours or overnight until set.

Garnish with whipped cream, chocolate curls, fresh berries or **raspberry coulis**. Serves 12 to 16.

Raspberry Coulis
6 cups fresh or frozen unsweetened raspberries
2/3 cup sugar or to taste
3 tablespoons cornstarch
1/4 cup water

Heat raspberries and sugar to boiling, strain well to discard seeds. Thicken with cornstarch mixed with water. Cool. Serve either under cheesecake on a plate or drizzle over top.

Bright House

RHUBARB CRISP
The Bright House

This rendition of an old fashioned fruit crisp is easy to prepare and a wonderful winter dessert. At the Bright House it is served with whipped cream!

3/4 cups rhubarb, chopped small
1/2 cup orange juice
3/4 cup sugar
1/2 teaspoon cinnamon
1 tablespoon butter
3/4 cup flour
3/4 cup brown sugar
3/4 cup rolled oats
3/4 cup flaked coconut
1/2 cup butter or margarine

Preheat oven to 350°F and grease a 9 x 9-inch baking dish. Combine rhubarb, orange juice and cinnamon and place in prepared pan. Dot with butter.

For the topping combine flour, sugar, rolled oats, coconut and butter with a pastry blender. Sprinkle over rhubarb. Bake until golden brown and bubbly, approximately 45 minutes.

Digby Neck

INDIVIDUAL CHEESECAKES WITH STRAWBERRY SAUCE
The Mountain Gap Inn

We tested these little cheesecakes at the height of the berry season. If you use frozen berries, we suggest you make a cooked sauce.

16 ounces cream cheese
1/3 teaspoon vanilla
2/3 cup sugar
4 teaspoons flour
dash of salt
zest and juice of 1 lemon
2 eggs
3 tablespoons blend
1 quart fresh strawberries, washed and hulled
1 tablespoon lemon juice
1/4 cup sugar, or to taste
1/2 cup heavy cream, whipped

Place cream cheese in a large mixing bowl and beat to soften. Add vanilla and sugar and beat until fluffy. Blend in flour and salt. Add lemon zest and juice and beat in eggs, one at a time. Beat in blend.

Grease 6 to 8 custard cups and line with plastic wrap. Fill three-quarters full with cheese mixture and place in a pan with 1/4-inch of water at the bottom. Bake at 350°F, until just set, about 20 minutes. Remove from oven and cool. Chill at least 2 hours before removing from cups.

For the sauce, prepare berries and slice into a bowl. Reserve 6 to 8 small berries for a garnish. Squeeze lemon juice over top and add sugar. Stir to coat and refrigerate a few hours, stirring occasionally.

To serve, unmold cheesecake onto serving plate. Spoon sauce over and garnish with whipped cream and small berries, if desired.

GERMAN RASPBERRY POUNDCAKE
The Braeside Inn

The Braeside serves this dessert warm with ice cream, whipped cream, fresh raspberries or raspberry sauce, but it may also be served cold.

1 cup butter
1 1/4 cup sugar
4 eggs, lightly beaten
1 3/4 cups flour
1 pint fresh raspberries

In a mixer, blend butter and sugar until creamy, about 3 minutes. Add egg and flour in three additions and whip at high speed for 7 minutes. Grease a 9-inch springform pan. Line the bottom with waxed paper and flour the sides. Spread half of the batter in the pan. Add the berries to form a uniform layer and spoon remaining batter over raspberries.

Bake in a preheated 350°F oven for approximately 1 hour or until cake leaves sides of pan and springs back when lightly touched in center.

VINEYARD'S CARROT TORTE
Chez La Vigne

Chef Alex Clavel says that this torte is better made two days before serving. It is even more succulent if carrots are grown in the vineyard!

5 egg yolks
1 1/2 cups sugar
lemon zest of 2 lemons
juice of 1 lemon
1/2 pound almonds, ground
1/2 pound carrots, finely grated
1/2 cup cornstarch
1/4 teaspoon cinnamon
1/4 teaspoon cloves
1 tablespoon baking powder
pinch of salt
5 egg whites, beaten to a stiff peak
3 1/2 tablespoons Kirsch
1/4 cup apricot jelly or puréed jam

Beat egg yolks, sugar, lemon juice and zest until thick and pale. Fold in almonds and grated carrots. Combine cornstarch, cinnamon, cloves, baking powder and salt. Mix lightly, but well, into batter. Fold egg whites and Kirsch into batter.

Line the bottom of a high, round 10-inch cake pan with oiled paper. Pour the batter into the pan and cook in a preheated 350°F oven for 1 hour or until centre springs back when lightly touched. Remove from the oven and while still hot, brush with apricot jelly. Glaze the torte with light royal icing or decorate with small marzipan carrots.

Captain Burgess Rum Cake (Blomidon Inn)

CAPTAIN BURGESS RUM CAKE
Blomidon Inn

This is probably the Blomidon Inn's best known dessert. Store your version for a day or two to let the rum flavour mellow.

3/4 cup softened butter
1 1/2 cups granulated sugar
4 large eggs
3 cups all purpose flour
1/4 teaspoon salt
4 1/2 teaspoons baking powder
1/2 cup dark rum
1 cup milk
1 cup raisins
1 cup chopped pecans
1/4 cup pecan halves
1/4 cup butter, melted
1/4 cup water
1 cup granulated sugar
1/4 cup dark rum

Grease a 10-inch tube pan and line with waxed paper.

Cream together butter and sugar until fluffy. Add eggs, one at a time, beating after each addition.

In a separate bowl, combine flour, salt and baking powder. Add dry ingredients to creamed mixture, alternately with rum and milk, being careful to mix only until batter is smooth. Fold in the raisins and chopped pecans.

Place halved pecans on the bottom of the tube pan. Spread the cake batter evenly over the nuts and bake at 350°F for 55 to 60 minutes, or until a toothpick inserted in center of the cake comes out clean. Turn the cake onto a rack to cool, before glazing.

In a small saucepan combine butter, water, sugar and rum and place over medium heat until sugar is dissolved. Prick the cake with a small skewer and drizzle the syrup over the cake until it is all absorbed. Store in a tightly sealed container at a cool temperature to mellow before serving. Yields 12 to 14 servings.

Avondale near Windsor, N.S.

HOT APPLE CAKE WITH CARAMEL PECAN SAUCE
St. Martins Country Inn

Desserts that have fruit or vegetables as ingredients, such as zucchini, carrot and apple cakes have a delicious flavour that improves if left for a day or two. This recipe with its accompanying pecan sauce will not likely survive that long.

1 cup unsalted butter, softened
1 cup sugar
2 eggs
1 teaspoon vanilla
1 1/2 cups all purpose flour
1 1/2 teaspoons cinnamon
1 teaspoon baking soda
1/4 teaspoon salt
4 medium tart apples, peeled, cored and finely
   chopped
3/4 cup pecans, coarsely chopped

In a mixer, cream butter and sugar until fluffy, approximately 3 minutes. On low speed, beat in eggs, one at a time and add vanilla.

Sift together dry ingredients and add to the batter, stirring just until mixed. Blend in apples and pecans.

Spoon batter into a greased 7 x 11-inch oblong cake pan and bake in a preheated 350°F oven for 35 to 45 minutes, until top is golden and a toothpick inserted in center of cake comes out clean. Cool in pan for 10 minutes before turning out on a rack.

Serve cake warm with vanilla ice-cream on the side and topped with **Caramel Pecan Sauce**.

Caramel Pecan Sauce
2 tablespoons unsalted butter
1/4 cup pecan halves
1/2 cup dark, brown sugar, packed
1/2 cup heavy cream (35% m.f.)
1 tablespoon bourbon or rum

In a small saucepan, over moderately-high heat, melt butter. Add nuts and cook, stirring constantly, until nuts are toasted and butter is light brown. Add sugar and cream. Continue to stir as sugar dissolves and the sauce boils, turning a deep golden brown. Remove from heat, add rum and cool.

Near Middleton in the Annapolis Valley

BLUEBERRY CAKE
Cobequid Inn

This is a cake that the whole family will enjoy. Served warm, cold or straight from the pan it will be gone before you know it.

1 cup butter
1 cup sugar
2 eggs
1/2 teaspoon lemon extract
2 cups all purpose flour
2 teaspoons baking powder
3/4 cup milk
1 cup blueberries, fresh or frozen
1/4 teaspoon cinnamon
3/4 cup brown sugar

Cream butter and sugar until light and fluffy. Beat in eggs and lemon extract. Sift flour and baking powder and add to batter alternately with milk, in two additions. Stir in blueberries and pour batter in 8 x 8-inch cake pan which has been lined with waxed paper. Combine cinnamon and brown sugar and sprinkle over batter.

Bake in a preheated 350°F oven for 35 to 45 minutes, until a toothpick inserted in the center of the cake comes out clean. Note, the cake takes the longer cooking time if using frozen berries.

RHUBARB COCONUT SQUARES
The Mountain Gap Inn

Chef Hank Lewis at Mountain Gap suggests that for these squares you leave the rhubarb filling rather tart because the topping is quite sweet.

Base
1 1/3 cups all purpose flour
1/2 cup unsalted butter
1/2 cup sugar
zest of 1/2 an orange

Filling
2 cups rhubarb, washed and diced
sugar to taste
juice of one orange
2 tablespoons butter
dash of freshly grated nutmeg

Topping
2 eggs
3/4 cup sugar (second amount)
2 1/2 cups long shredded coconut
1 1/2 teaspoon vanilla
2 tablespoons flour
zest of half an orange

Blend together the first 4 ingredients until mealy. Spread evenly in a greased 9 x 9-inch pan and press down firmly.

Boil together rhubarb, sugar and orange juice until the mixture thickens. Remove from the heat and stir in butter and nutmeg. Allow to cool slightly and then spread over crust.

For the topping, blend together eggs, sugar, coconut, vanilla, flour and zest. Spread over filling and bake squares at 350°F until lightly browned, about 25 to 30 minutes. Allow to cool before cutting into squares.

MAPLE MOUSSE
Loon Bay Lodge

The chef at Loon Bay Lodge admits that all this cream is bad for the heart, but tells us, "It is oh so good for the soul."

3 eggs, separated
3/4 cup pure maple syrup
1/3 teaspoon vanilla
1 cup heavy cream (35% m.f.)
Whipped cream and toasted slivered almonds
    for garnish

Beat egg yolks and blend in maple syrup. Place mixture in a heavy saucepan and cook over low heat, stirring constantly, until it reaches the consistency of soft custard, about 10 minutes. Remove from heat, add vanilla and cool.

Whip cream and fold into cooled custard. Beat egg whites until stiff and fold into custard. Pour into parfait glasses and freeze until firm.

Let stand at room temperature for 10 to 15 minutes before serving. Garnish with whipped cream and toasted almond slivers, if desired. Serves 6.

CRANACHAN
Glenora Inn and Distillery

This traditional Scottish dessert, known also as "Fardach", was served locally on Hallowe'en. A wedding ring or button was stirred into the dessert. Family and friends would each take a spoon and eat from the same bowl. The lucky one to retrieve the ring would be the next to marry.

3/4 cup oatmeal, toasted
1 1/2 cups heavy cream (35% m.f.)
1/3 cup icing sugar, sifted
3/4 teaspoon vanilla
fresh blueberries
2 ounces dark rum

Place oatmeal on a baking sheet and cook in a preheated 350°F oven until golden, about 6 to 8 minutes; cool and reserve. Whip cream with sugar and vanilla until firm. Stir in cooled oatmeal. Spoon mixture into four serving dishes and top with fresh blueberries (or fresh fruit of choice). Garnish with fresh mint or a lime twist and drizzle 1/2 ounce of rum over top. The Glenora Inn uses Smuggler's Cove, their own brand of rum. Serves 4.

MAPLE SUGAR CRÈME BRULÉE
Dalvay-by-the-Sea

For a lighter crème brulée you may substitute milk or blend (12% m.f.) or any combination of milk, blend and cream for the heavy cream in this recipe. Dalvay-by-the-Sea accompanies this dessert with sugared almond cookies.

1/2 cup maple syrup
2 cups heavy cream (35% m.f.)
1/2 vanilla bean, split or 1/2 teaspoon vanilla
    extract
zest of 1/2 lemon, cut fine
1/2 cinnamon stick, crushed
6 egg yolks
1 1/2 teaspoon sugar

Bring maple syrup to a boil. Simmer for 2 minutes, remove from heat and let cool. In a saucepan, slowly bring cream, vanilla, lemon zest and cinnamon to a boil. Meanwhile, beat yolks and sugar until thick and pale in colour. Whisk boiling cream mixture into yolks. Return mixture to saucepan and stir over low heat until thick.

Strain cream into a cold bowl which is set in ice and whisk rapidly. Fold maple syrup into the chilled custard. Fill small chilled *pots de crème*, or custard cups, to rim and refrigerate overnight. Before serving, sprinkle white sugar and spray a light coat of water on top of creams. Place custards under a preheated broiler to brown. Serve immediately. Serves 4.

Garrison House

STRAWBERRIES WITH CITRUS RIESLING SABAYON
The Garrison House Inn

There is nothing to compare to the sweet juicy taste of your first strawberry of the season. Unless of course you choose to try this superb recipe from Patrick Redgrave's kitchen. The winner will be hard to choose.

3 egg yolks
3 tablespoons sugar
2 teaspoons mixed orange/lemon zest (thinly cut peel)
1/2 cup Riesling wine
1/3 cup heavy cream (35% m.f.)
2 teaspoons Cointreau (or other orange liqueur)
1 quart fresh strawberries, hulled
2 tablespoons dark bitter chocolate, grated
sprigs of mint leaves

Beat egg yolks, sugar and citrus zest until thick, about 5 minutes. Put yolk mixture in top of a double boiler over simmering water, and gradually whisk in the wine. Continue whisking until the mixture will stick to the back of a spoon, approximately 7 minutes. Remove from heat and cool mixture over a bowl of ice water.

Whip cream and liqueur and fold into chilled sabayon. Arrange berries in dessert dishes and spoon sabayon over them. Dust with grated chocolate and garnish with fresh mint. Serves 4.

BREAD AND BUTTER PUDDING WITH STRAWBERRY SAUCE
La Poissonnière

Remember the bread puddings from your grandmother's kitchen? Richard Chiasson's modern version will satisfy the most discriminating palate.

2 cups strawberries, cleaned and sliced
1/2 cup sugar (for sauce)
1 teaspoon cornstarch
3 teaspoons cold water
9 slices of stale bread
1/4 cup soft butter
4 eggs
3 tablespoons sugar

Annapolis Royal Gardens

1/4 teaspoon vanilla
1/4 teaspoon salt
2 1/2 cups milk, scalded
cinnamon and nutmeg for garnish

Prepare strawberries and place in a bowl. Add 1/2 cup of sugar and let sit, refrigerated, 24 hours. Drain juice from berries into a small saucepan and set over medium heat until it begins to boil. Combine cornstarch and water and add to strawberry juice. Once thickened, remove from heat and cool. Add strawberries.

Preheat oven to 350°F. Butter each slice of bread, then cut into 1/2 inch squares. Grease 6 individual ramekin dishes and divide bread cubes between them. In a mixing bowl combine eggs, sugar, vanilla and salt. Gradually stir in hot, scalded milk, then pour mixture over bread pieces. Sprinkle with nutmeg and cinnamon. Set dishes in a pan containing 1 inch of hot water. Bake 35 to 40 minutes or until set. Invert onto serving plates, and serve hot or cold with strawberry sauce. At La Poissonnière patrons are treated to whipped cream! Serves 6.

Strathgartney Country Inn

ORANGE YOGHURT MOUSSE
The Normaway Inn

When we asked Chef Ryan Nicholson for a low-fat dessert he immediately produced this winner. It is easy to prepare, healthy and is refreshingly tasty.

1 envelope unflavoured gelatin
1/4 cup warm water
4 tablespoons sugar (optional, 4 packets of
    Nutrasweet)
2 cups fresh orange juice reduced to 1/2 cup
    or 1/2 cup frozen orange juice concentrate
2 cups low-fat unflavoured yoghurt
1 1/2 cups fruit (raspberries, strawberries,
    blueberries etc.)
1 tablespoon sugar (2nd amount)
1 teaspoon fresh lemon juice

Sprinkle gelatin over water and let stand for 5 minutes to soften. Heat allusion over low heat until it dissolves. Add sugar and stir to dissolve.

If using fresh orange juice, reduce over medium heat to 1/2 cup. Pour orange juice into a bowl and briskly whisk in the yoghurt, being careful not to over process. Stir in gelatin mixture. Pour mousse into 4 parfait glasses or 6 ramekins and refrigerate until set.

Combine fruit, sugar (2nd amount) and lemon juice in a food processor and purée. Strain purée through a fine sieve and refrigerate.

To serve, pour fruit purée over desserts and garnish with fresh mint. Serves 4 to 6.

CRÈME CARAMEL
Strathgartney Country Inn

Prepare your crème caramels early in the day so that they are well chilled before being turned out on the serving plates.

Caramel glaze
1/2 cup sugar
1 1/2 tablespoons water

Custard
2 cups milk
3/4 cup confectioners' sugar
2 egg yolks
4 whole eggs
1 teaspoon vanilla
Fresh fruit, as garnish (optional)

Have ready 6 lightly greased custard cups.

Heat sugar for caramel glaze in a saucepan. Begin to stir when it starts to melt around the edges, then stir slowly but continuously. When it is fully melted, cautiously stir in the water all at once. Divide caramel evenly among custard cups.

Heat milk and sugar until almost boiling. In a large bowl, combine yolks and whole eggs, then gradually stir in the hot milk. Strain into custard cups. Place custard cups in pan with 1/4 inch of water. Bake at 400°F for 20 minutes.

Let the custard cool thoroughly, then run a knife around the inside of the cup before unmolding on serving plate. Garnish with fresh fruit.

Strathgartney Country Inn

Acton's Stoneground Wholewheat Bread

BREADS

Breads, rolls or muffins accompany most meals in Maritime cuisine and this is a small sampling of some of our best recipes. While some directions are time consuming, we feel that all could be prepared with excellent results by a novice cook.

Acton's *Stoneground Wholewheat Bread* and *Maritime Brown Bread* from the Compass Rose on Grand Manan Island in New Brunswick are yeast breads and obviously take time to prepare. Nicholas Pierce of *Acton's Grill and Café* buys his stoneground wholewheat flour from a local farm and the *Maritime Brown Bread* includes the traditional ingredients of molasses and rolled oats.

Also included are a number of healthy and easily prepared quick breads. Golden yellow *Corn Bread* from MacAskill's Restaurant is a wonderful accompaniment to hearty winter meals while *Purple Violet Bread* from Shirley Ayles' kitchen at the Aylesford Inn includes wild violets for taste and decoration.

Acton's Stoneground Wholewheat Bread

ACTON'S STONEGROUND WHOLEWHEAT BREAD
Acton's Grill and Café

The bread at Acton's is made daily and is so popular with guests that they often ask for a second basket to be brought to the table.

2 fresh yeast cakes or 2 packages active dry
   yeast
2 cups warm water
1 tablespoon sugar
1 tablespoon salt
1 tablespoon olive oil (or vegetable oil)
2 to 2 1/2 cups all purpose flour
3 cups wholewheat flour (preferably
   stoneground)

Dissolve the yeast in the warm water along with the sugar, salt and oil. Add 1 cup of all purpose flour and whisk together well. Let this "sponge" proof for 45 minutes in a warm place.

Add remaining flours and work into a soft but not sticky dough. Depending on the quality of the flour, you may need a little more to get desired consistency. Place dough in a lightly greased bowl, turning once to grease surface. Cover and let rise, in a warm place, until double in size, about 1 hour.

Punch down dough and form into 2 free-form oval loaves. Place on greased cookie sheet, cover and let rise again, until doubled, about 45 minutes. Bake in preheated 400°F oven for 25 to 30 minutes. Bread is cooked if hollow sounding when tapped on bottom. Brush tops with melted butter if desired. Makes two large loaves.

Acton's Grill and Café

122

CORNMEAL BREAD
MacAskill's Restaurant

Cornmeal gives a lovely flavour and colour to breads and muffins and this recipe is no exception. The recipe makes two large loaves, one to savour while it is still warm and one to freeze for a busy day.

1 2/3 cups cornmeal
2 cups water
1 1/2 cups sugar
3/4 cup shortening
1 1/2 teaspoons salt
3 eggs
3 1/2 cups flour
1/3 cup whey powder (or skim milk powder)
2 tablespoons baking powder

Soak cornmeal in water in a bowl. In a mixer, cream sugar, shortening and salt until light and fluffy. Add eggs, one at a time. Sift together flour, whey powder and baking powder. Add to batter, mixing until dry ingredients are just incorporated. Slowly add cornmeal, scraping bowl often, until it is completely blended. Increase speed and beat for 2 minutes.

Grease and flour two 8 x 4-inch loaf pans and divide batter between them. Bake in preheated 350°F oven for 45 to 50 minutes until a toothpick inserted in center comes out clean. Makes 2 loaves.

Cornmeal Bread (MacAskill's Restaurant)

Hole-in-the-Wall at Grand Manan

MARITIME BROWN BREAD
The Compass Rose, N.B.

Truly a traditional Maritime bread, this molasses laced brown bread recipe makes two loaves and is a pleasant accompaniment to a hearty meal.

1 cup rolled oats
2 teaspoons salt
2 tablespoons lard
1/2 cup molasses
2 cups boiling water
1 package yeast
1/2 cup warm water
1 teaspoon molasses (2nd amount)
5 cups white flour

In a large bowl combine rolled oats, salt, lard, molasses and boiling water and stir until lard dissolves. Cool to lukewarm.

Stir 1 teaspoon molasses into 1/2 cup lukewarm water, sprinkle yeast over top and stir to dissolve. When yeast has doubled in size, add to rolled oats mixture. Stir in flour, a cupful at a time. Turn onto a floured board and knead until smooth, 4 to 5 minutes. Shape into a ball and place in a lightly greased bowl, turning once to grease surface. Cover and let rise in a warm place until double, about 1 hour.

Punch down dough, divide in half and shape into two loaves. Place in greased 9 x 5-inch pans. Cover and let rise about 1 hour.

Bake in a preheated 350°F oven, 30 to 40 minutes. Remove from pans and cool on wire racks. Yields 2 loaves.

DOWN DRURY LANE WHITE ROLLS
Drury Lane Steak House

At Drury Lane these rolls are served hot with steaming bowls of chowder. They are economical, easy to prepare and good enough to make this a basic recipe for your files.

2 teaspoons sugar
1/2 cup lukewarm water
1 1/2 tablespoons dry yeast (1 1/2 packages)
3 cups hot water
1/4 cup shortening
1 tablespoon salt

1 tablespoon sugar
8 to 9 cups all purpose flour

Dissolve sugar in warm water. Sprinkle yeast over top and let stand in a warm place for 10 to 15 minutes. In a large bowl, add shortening, salt and sugar to hot water. Stir and let cool while the yeast is proofing. When the hot water has cooled to 85°F, whisk in the yeast mixture. Stir in flour, 2 cups at a time, until you cannot stir any more. Let the batter rest for 10 minutes.

Turn batter onto a floured surface and knead, adding more flour as necessary to prevent sticking, until, as the chef says, "'the cows come home," approximately 10 to 12 minutes. Place dough in a greased bowl, turn to coat, cover and let rise until doubled in size, 1 to 1 1/2 hours. Punch down dough, shape into rolls and place in greased muffin tins. Cover and let rise for 30 minutes, until doubled. Bake in a preheated 350°F oven for 15 minutes or until golden brown. Remove from oven. Brush with melted butter and immediately remove from pans. Makes 3 1/2 to 4 dozen.

NOVA SCOTIA OATCAKES
The Palliser

It is said that Scottish settlers brought their recipe for oatcakes to Canada's shores. The twentieth-century version continues to be popular with everyone, regardless of its country of origin.

1 1/2 cups flour
1/4 teaspoon soda
1/4 teaspoon baking powder
generous dash of salt
1 1/2 cups oatmeal
1/2 cup brown sugar
1/2 cup shortening
1/2 cup butter or margarine
2 1/2 tablespoons water
1/4 teaspoon vanilla

Mix the dry ingredients in a large bowl. Cut in shortening and butter with pastry blender. Add water and vanilla. Roll out on a floured surface to 1/4-inch thickness. Cut in squares and place on a greased cookie sheet. Bake at 375°F for 10 to 12 minutes, until golden brown. Yields 12 to 16 oatcakes.

NUT AND SEEDS BREAD
Bluenose Lodge

Bluenose Lodge owners Ron and Grace Swan serve this healthy bread accompanied by Liptauer cheese during the town of Lunenburg's annual Oktoberfest. The loaf keeps very well, wrapped and refrigerated.

2 1/4 cups white flour
3/4 cup whole wheat flour
1 1/2 teaspoons baking powder
1 1/2 teaspoons baking soda
3/4 teaspoon salt
1 1/2 cups brown sugar, lightly packed
1/2 cup chopped nuts (walnuts, pecans etc.)
3 tablespoons wheat germ
3 tablespoons sesame seeds
3 tablespoons poppy seeds
2 eggs
1/3 cup + 1 tablespoon vegetable oil
1 1/2 cups buttermilk

In a large bowl combine all dry ingredients and mix thoroughly. In a separate bowl beat together eggs, oil and buttermilk. Add liquid to dry ingredients and stir until just mixed. Pour batter into a greased and floured 9 x 5-inch loaf pan. Bake in a preheated 350°F oven for 55 to 60 minutes or until a tester inserted in center of loaf, comes out clean. Cool a few minutes and then turn out on wire rack.

PURPLE VIOLET BREAD
Aylesford Inn

The purple violet is the floral emblem of New Brunswick, adopted in 1936 at the request of the Women's Institute. How fitting for Shirley Ayles to incorporate this beautiful and edible flower into her tea bread.

3 cups all purpose flour
1 cup white sugar
1 tablespoon baking powder
1/2 teaspoon salt
1/4 teaspoon baking soda
1 egg
1 2/3 cups milk
1/4 cup vegetable oil
1/2 cup walnuts, chopped
3 tablespoons violet flowers
2 tablespoons brown sugar

In a large bowl, stir together flour, white sugar, baking powder, salt and baking soda. Beat together egg, milk and oil and add to the flour mixture, stirring just until combined. Set aside 10 of the violets. Gently stir the walnuts and remaining violets into the batter.

Divide batter into two greased 7 1/2 x 3 1/2-inch loaf pans. Gently press reserved violets into the batter in each pan and sprinkle tops with brown sugar. Bake in a preheated 350°F oven for 40 to 45 minutes, until a toothpick inserted in centre of bread comes out clean. Cool in pans for 10 minutes, remove and cool on wire racks.

May be served warm or cool. Makes 2 loaves.

Bluenose Lodge

BERRY LAYER MUFFINS
Auberge Le Heron Country Inn

You can use whatever fruit is in season to give these wonderful little muffins a change of flavour. Make a double batch and freeze half to enjoy later.

1/3 cup butter
2/3 cup brown sugar
2 eggs
3/4 cup milk
1/2 teaspoon vanilla
2 cups flour
4 teaspoons baking powder
1/2 teaspoon salt
3/4 cup fresh whole berries (for example, blueberries, raspberries)
2 tablespoons sugar
1 teaspoon cinnamon

Cream together butter and brown sugar until fluffy. Beat in eggs, milk and vanilla; don't be alarmed if mixture curdles.

Sift together flour, baking powder and salt and add, all at once to creamed mixture stirring just enough to dampen dry ingredients.

Grease 12 large muffin tins and fill halfway with batter. Place a heaping spoonful of berries in centre of batter and fill tins with remaining batter. Combine sugar and cinnamon and sprinkle over muffins. Bake in preheated 375°F oven for 20 to 25 minutes. Makes 1 dozen large muffins.

CRANBERRY ORANGE MUFFINS
The Mountain Gap Inn

The chef at Mountain Gap Inn generously shared her recipe for these tart little muffins. Double your batch because they freeze well!

1 cup cranberries, coarsely chopped
1 egg, beaten
2/3 cup milk
1/3 cup butter, melted
3 tablespoons orange juice concentrate
1/2 teaspoon vanilla
zest of 1 orange
1 3/4 cups all purpose flour
2 1/2 teaspoons baking powder
1/3 cup sugar
1 teaspoon salt

Mix together cranberries, egg, milk, butter, orange juice, vanilla and zest. In a bowl, sift together the flour and baking powder and stir in the sugar and salt. Add the milk mixture to the dry ingredients, stirring just enough to blend. Spoon into paper lined muffin tins and bake at 400°F until golden, 20 to 25 minutes. Yields 12 muffins.

NEW BRUNSWICK

Be prepared to leave the main arterial highways as you travel around New Brunswick, the largest of the three Maritime provinces. Canada's "picture province" lives up to its name and the inns and restaurants we have featured are nestled amid the forests and along the shores of this photographer's paradise.

Waterford, near Sussex, N.B.

THE ALGONQUIN

Atop a hill overlooking the historic town of St. Andrews lies the Algonquin Resort Hotel, a massive turreted structure featuring more than 200 guest rooms, tennis, swimming, cycling, golf and superb cuisine in five restaurants.

The resort town of St. Andrews was founded by United Empire Loyalists in 1783, many of the first residents having dismantled their homes in Maine to reassemble them across Passamaquoddy Bay in New Brunswick. More than half of the

The Algonquin

town's buildings are over 100 years old, and a walking tour of the streets is a pleasant way to spend a morning. Other attractions of St. Andrews include the Huntsman Marine Science Aquarium-Museum, with its "please touch, tank", West Point Blockhouse, boat tours of the bay and whale-watching cruises. From nearby St. George, a car ferry operates seasonally to Deer Island where another ferry transports you to Campobello Island, site of the Roosevelt International Park and summer home of the late President Franklin Delano Roosevelt.

Season: May through October
Major credit cards
Manager: Barry Zwueste
St. Andrews by the Sea, NB
E0G 2X0
1-800-563-4299

AUBERGE LE VIEUX PRESBYTÈRE DE BOUCTOUCHE 1880

The "Vieux Presbytère" is a comfortable Acadian inn built in 1880 as a rectory, enlarged as years passed to become a retreat house and a nursing home. Recently renovated, the inn contains a collection of 22 rooms and suites. All menu planning is carried out by Marcelle Albert, *chef de cuisine*. The banquet room, formerly a chapel, with vaulted ceilings and a choir loft, accommodates 125. The dining room, "Le Tire-bouchon" (The Corkscrew), seats 45 and offers the best of regional cuisine. As well, an innovative wine cellar is set up to host small wine-tasting groups, and upon request, can serve meals to a maximum of 12 people.

Nearby, one finds the famous Pays de la Sagouine, a park dedicated to the fictional

Cape Tormentine lighthouse

AYLESFORD INN

The Aylesford Inn of Campbellton is one of the finest examples of Victorian architecture in New Brunswick. Built at the turn of the century by John Murray Maclean, this warm and gracious home has elegant stained-glass windows, elaborate woodwork and cabinets with leaded glass doors. In keeping with its character, the 7 guest rooms are furnished with period antiques.

Guests are invited to enjoy the gardens and grounds, or to sit on the wrap-around verandah in the shade of chestnut and lilac trees. Breakfast is served to overnight guests, afternoon tea to the public on Monday, Wednesday and Friday, and dinner to the public by advance reservation.

Open year round
Major credit cards
Innkeeper: Shirley Keays Ayles
8 MacMillan Avenue
Campbellton, NB
E3N 1E9
(506) 759-7672

characters of Acadian author Antonine Maillet. A visit to the park is an immersion in the lifestyle, music and history of the "land of Acadie." Overlooking Bouctouche Bay, La Vieux Presbytère De Bouctouche 1880 is 30 minutes from Moncton and 25 minutes from the warm sandy beaches, trails and wildlife of Kouchibouguac National Park.

Season: May to October
Visa and MasterCard
Manager: Louise Michaud
157 Chemin du Couvent
P.O. Box 479
Bouctouche, N.B.
E0A 1G0
(506) 743-5568

Chez Françoise

CHEZ FRANÇOISE

Chez Françoise opened to the public in 1982 in a property known locally as "Elmbank" or the Tait House. The Taits arrived from Scotland around 1875 and became prosperous merchants. The inn, built in 1911, offers 19 rooms. Guests may relax in the peaceful sitting rooms or large cool verandahs that overlook Shediac Bay.

Gourmet dining, specializing in seafood with a French flavour, is offered to guests and the public in the inn's fireside diningroom. Highlights of the menu include salmon, halibut, shrimp or crab, all prepared with the freshest ingredients.

Located at Shediac, a short drive from Moncton, Chez Françoise is close to the warm waters of the Northumberland Strait. This area of New Brunswick is an ideal destination for vacationers who enjoy water sports and beaches.

Season: May through December
Major credit cards
Innkeepers: Jacques and Helene Cadieux Johanny
P. O. Box 715
Shediac, NB
E0A 3G0
(506) 532-4233

THE COMPASS ROSE

The Compass Rose is located on Grand Manan, an isolated island of steep cliffs and secluded beaches, 21/2 hours offshore in the Bay of Fundy. Easily accessible by ferry from Blacks Harbour, the island is a haven for artists, hikers, birdwatchers and photographers.

The inn, situated close to the ferry wharf at North Head, consists of 2 charming houses offering accommodation in 9 guest rooms. Breakfast, lunch and dinner are served in the dining room which opens to a long deck overlooking the harbour. All dishes are prepared at the inn and feature local produce and fresh seafood from the Bay of Fundy.

Season: May through October
Visa
Innkeeper: Cecilia Bowden
North Head
Grand Manan Island, NB
E0G 2M0
(506) 662-8570

DRURY LANE STEAK HOUSE

Drury Lane Steak House is a small restaurant adjacent to Fort Beausejour National Historic Park, at Aulac. The original building was built 220 years ago by an officer of the fort so that his wife and family could follow him to the New World from France. Local lore tells us that she only stayed three months! We can only assume that they were harsh winter months, because spring, summer and autumn are delightful seasons in this area of New Brunswick.

The dining room overlooks the Tantramar Marshes and Chignecto Basin, an area renowned for birdwatching. Polished pine floors and hand-hewn beams, accented by red-and-white checked curtains and table linens, set a scene of rustic tranquility. Drury Lane offers chowders, crusty rolls, fresh seafood entrées and homemade desserts prepared daily on the premises.

The restaurant is open for lunch and dinner.

Season: mid-May to mid-October
Major credit cards
Restaurateur: Sharon Meldrum
P.O.Box 1720
Sackville, NB
E0A 3C0
(506) 536-1252

DUFFERIN INN & SAN MARTELLO DINING ROOM

Margret and Axel Begner have turned the historic home of J.B.M. Baxter, former Premier of New Brunswick, into a peaceful haven which offers a superb dining experience.

The Inn, tucked under the historic San Martello Tower in central Saint John, features gracious accommodations in its nine non-smoking guest rooms. Full breakfast is included in the price for lodging. The Begners, who immigrated to Canada from Germany, have had extensive restaurant experience. At the San Martello Room you can expect to find an innovative and changing menu offering traditional and European dishes and sumptuous desserts, all prepared with freshest of additive free products.

Open year round
Visa and MasterCard
Closed Mondays
Reservations required for dinner
Innkeepers: Margret & Axel Begner
357 Dufferin Row
Saint John, NB E2M 2J7
(506) 635-5968

GASTON'S RESTAURANT

Gaston's, located on the main floor of the Blue Cross Centre in the heart of downtown Moncton, has an extensive lunch and dinner menu. Owner Gaston Frigault offers seafood prepared in a variety of cooking styles, as well as steaks and daily entrée specials.

Patrons may dine in a bar and eating area with plants and cosy upholstered booths, or in the main restaurant with large glassed walls that offer a view of streetside activities.

Open year round
Major credit cards
Restaurateur: Gaston Frigault
644 rue Main Street
Moncton, NB
E1C 1E2
(506) 858-8998

INN ON THE COVE

This small inn, perched at the banks of the Bay of Fundy offers a serene pastoral setting while only five minutes from the centre of the busy city of Saint John. You can enjoy the cosy firelit rooms and revel in the radiance of moonlight dancing across the water to the flashing of Partridge Island light.

The inn features five guest rooms, each with private bath and some with whirlpool tub or gas fireplace. Breakfast is complimentary, and a five course dinner is available to guests and the public with advance notice, Tuesday through Saturday. Nature lovers can request a picnic lunch to enjoy at the beach or on a short stroll. Nearby, one can visit Saint's Rest Marsh hosts 240 species of birds and is a crucial staging ground in the Atlantic flyway.

Open year round
MasterCard and Visa
Innkeepers: Ross and Willa Mavis
1371 Sand Cove Road
P.O.Box 3113 Station B
Saint John, NB E2M 4X7
(506) 672-7799

LA POISSONNIÈRE RESTAURANT

Warm hospitality and *joie de vivre* await you at La Poissonnière, a restaurant located at Grande-Anse, on the Acadian Coast in northeastern New Brunswick. The dining room is open for breakfast, lunch and dinner daily. Husband and wife team, Ronda Jen and Richard Chiasson, prepare a menu of superb seafood and Acadian cuisine.

Local attractions include the Shippagan Marine Centre, Miscou Island and the Acadian Historical Village, a recreated settlement at Caraquet. At the village you can watch "residents" carry out the tasks of yesteryear, such as weaving, carding wool and soapmaking. For those seeking a relaxing vacation, the Bay of Chaleur area offers touring, beaches, birdwatching and beachcombing.

Season: Father's Day to September
Major credit cards
Restaurateur: Richard Chiasson
484 Acadie Street
Grande-Anse, NB
E0B 1R0
(506) 732-2000

LOON BAY LODGE

Originally built for New York Metropolitan Opera star Richard Crooks, Loon Bay Lodge overlooks the Saint-Croix, a Canadian Heritage River on the New Brunswick–Maine international border. Outdoor activities such as guided whitewater canoeing, fishing, photography and swimming abound at this private 200-acre retreat.

The dining room features traditional New Brunswick foods prepared on the premises. Accommodations are available in 9 guest rooms, each highlighted by a stone fireplace.

Loon Bay Lodge is an ideal destination for couples, families or corporate groups who enjoy comfort in a natural setting.

Season: May to November
Visa
Innkeepers: David and Judy Whittingham
P.O. Box 101
St. Stephen, NB
E3L 2W9
(506) 466-1240

MARSHLANDS INN

Marshlands Inn, located in Sackville, is comprised of two stately manors plus a coach house, offering 20 antique furnished guest rooms. This peaceful and tranquil establishment features nooks, dormer windows and fireside seats for reading and relaxation.

The dining room at Marshlands offers a wide choice of meals including home-prepared patés, creamy chowders as well as hearty fare such as steak and roast beef.

The inn takes its name from the Tantramar Marshes that surround the town. This area is along one of the main North American flyways for bird migration and provides the opportunity to view many species of birds as they come to rest on the marshy flats each spring and fall.

Open year round
Major credit cards
Innkeeper: Peter and Dianne Weedon
P. O. Box 1440
Sackville, NB
E0A 3C0
(506) 536-0170

PARKERHOUSE INN

Parkerhouse Inn is a restored Victorian mansion situated in downtown Saint John. This elegant brick home was built in 1890 by 28-year-old Dr. Walter Woodworth White for his betrothed, Nellie Troop. Fearing the good doctor was too old, Nellie broke the engagement; but three years later, she had a change of heart and the couple were married. Nellie and Walter had four children and lived happily, in their Sydney Street home, for 59 years, until Walter's death at eighty-nine.

The elegant, yet comfortable ambience of the Whites' home lives on today in the Parkerhouse Inn. Cautious restoration has preserved the beautiful stained glass-windows, circular solarium and original woodwork. The inn offers 9 antique decorated bedrooms and suites, each with private bath. Rates include free parking and a full breakfast.

The Parkerhouse Inn operates a licensed dining room, offering fine cuisine, to guests and the general public, for dinner.

Open year round
Visa, MasterCard and American Express
Innkeeper: Pamela Vincent
71 Sydney Street,
Saint John, NB
E2L 2L5
(506) 652-5054

QUACO INN

Picturesque St. Martins is home to Quaco Inn, a stately mansion situated just yards from the Bay of Fundy. Built by the Skillen family, local merchants in the early days of sail and shipbuilding, this old home reflects those prosperous times.

The inn provides hearty breakfasts to guests and dinner to guests and the public by advance reservation. The rooms, each with private bath, are named after former shipbuilding families of the area. In fact, each room is decorated with photographs and furniture from the homes of its namesake.

St. Martins is New Brunswick's "well kept secret." Less than one hour's drive from Saint John, the village borders a 3 1/2-mile beach featuring unique rock formations, caves and stretches of sand. A visit to the Quaco Inn is ideal for sunbathing, birdwatching, sketching and relaxing.

Open year round
Visa and MasterCard
Innkeeper: Katherine
Landry
Beach Street
St. Martins, NB
E0G 2Z0
(506) 833-4772

THE ROSSMOUNT INN

At Rossmount you step back in time to the romantic Victorian era. The inn, a three-storey manor house with 18 guest rooms, is part of a private 97-acre estate at the foot of Chamcook Mountain, overlooking the Passamaquoddy Bay.

The property provides scenic hiking, nature trails, a large pool and spectacular panoramic views.

The inn's dining room provides superb home cooked food and a good selection of wines. The Victorian decor is complemented by high ceilings and a fine old fireplace, but the focal point is an alcove of three stained-glass windows taken from an eighteenth-century English chapel.

At Rossmount, the rooms are distinctive and spacious, furnished with antiques from all over

the world. The menu features fresh seafood and several meat entrées.

Season: May through October
Visa and MasterCard
Innkeepers: Webber and Alice Burns
St. Andrews by the Sea, NB
E0G 2X0
(506)529-3351

SHADOW LAWN COUNTRY INN

Nestled near the Kennebecasis River at Rothesay, this multi-roomed Victorian structure was built in 1871 as a summer home by Saint John merchant James E. Robertson.

The Shadow Lawn Country Inn offers overnight accommodations in 8 elegantly appointed guest rooms. The mahogany-panelled lounge, sitting rooms and dining room are large and inviting. Dinner and breakfast are served to guests as well as the general public by advance reservation only. In addition, the lawns, gardens and patio make the inn an ideal place for

receptions and special-occasion events.

Open year round
Major credit cards
Innkeepers: Patrick and Margaret Gallagher
P. O. Box 41
Rothesay, NB
E0G 2W0
(506) 847-7539

STEAMERS STOP INN

Steamers Stop Inn in Gagetown is a charming colonial-style inn, offering accommodations in 7 guest rooms. The dining room, with its several

St. John River near Gagetown

quaint areas, is a place to enjoy traditional New Brunswick fare.

Located on scenic route 102, 65 miles north of Saint John and 40 miles south of the capital city of Fredericton, Gagetown boasts many attractions, including weavers, potters and several craft emporiums. History buffs can visit

the Queens County Museum, which occupies the house where "Father of Confederation" Samuel Leonard Tilley was born in 1818, or stroll among the moss-covered tombstones of Loyalists in the Anglican churchyard.

Because of its location on the banks of the Saint John River, Steamers Stop Inn is accessible to both the boating and motoring public. The inn can accommodate group parties and is an excellent getaway for small business meetings.

Season: Mother's Day through mid-October
Visa and MasterCard
Innkeeper: Vic and Pat Stewart
P.O. Box 155
Village of Gagetown, NB
E0G 1V0
(506) 488-2903

ST. MARTINS COUNTRY INN

Built in 1857, this replica of a Queen Anne villa was home to the William Vaughan family. At that time, St. Martins was a prosperous shipbuilding and trading centre. Today, this tranquil fishing port provides an ideal retreat from the hustle and bustle of modern times. Visitors can experience nature at its best, amid covered bridges, gingerbread clapboard homes and the brightly painted fishing boats that grace the Fundy shoreline.

The St. Martins Country Inn provides guests with the elegant ambience one would expect to find in what the locals refer to as "the castle". The antique furnished dining room offers fine cuisine to guests and the public. Patrons will be offered delicious ginger muffins at breakfast and an array of appetizers, entrées and desserts to choose from at dinner.

Open year round
Visa and MasterCard
Innkeepers: Myrna and Albert LeClair
R R #1
St. Martins, NB
E0G 2Z0
1-800-565-5257

NOVA SCOTIA

In Nova Scotia, with its thousands of miles of coastline, one is always less than an hour's drive from the sea. This is a province of geographical and cultural contrasts and we found these diversities mirrored in the province's inns and restaurants.

ACTON'S GRILL AND CAFÉ

In 1991 Nicholas Pearce and David Barrett sold their popular Toronto restaurant, Fenton's, and moved their culinary expertise to the peaceful Annapolis Valley town of Wolfville. Here they created Acton's, an upscale eatery, casually decorated with artwork, antique ceramics and, as you step through the threshold, an ever changing, giant bouquet of fresh flowers.

Acton's prides itself on creating recipes that use fresh local ingredients, such as Valley

produce and Bay of Fundy seafood. The menu is varied and offers patrons their choice of cuisine, from low calorie, "heart-smart" dishes to more decadent fare. The three pastas featured on the menu are classified Light, Not So Light and Rich; the choice is yours.

Open daily for lunch and dinner from 11:30 a.m.
Major credit cards
Restaurateurs: Nicholas Pearce and David Barrett
268 Main Street,
Wolfville, NS,
B0P 1X0
(902) 542-7525

AMHERST SHORE COUNTRY INN

Located on the shores of Northumberland Strait in northeastern Nova Scotia, this small inn (above right) offers accommodation in its guest rooms or beach side cottages. Dinner is available to guests and the public at a 7:30 sitting, by advance reservations only.

Everything is prepared on premises and innkeeper Donna Laceby makes excellent use of the inn's extensive gardens. The menu changes each day with a choice of meat or seafood entrée and either a rich or light dessert. The first person to make dinner reservations helps decide what will be served that evening.

There are 25 small-craft harbours along the Northumberland Shore where visitors may fish from the wharves or watch the lobster boats return. Locals boast that their numerous beaches have the warmest waters north of the Carolinas.

Inland sidetrips could include a visit to the Balmoral Grist Mill or the Sutherland Steam Mill. Both are open to the public and are situated amid the fertile farmlands of rural Nova Scotia.

Season: May through mid October
Major credit cards
Innkeepers: James and Donna Laceby
RR#2 Amherst,
Lorneville, NS,
B4H 3X9
(902) 661-4800

BELLHILL TEA HOUSE AND GIFT SHOP

Betty Rockwell and Wilma Gibson have been offering their patrons fine food in a friendly casual atmosphere for over ten years. This little blue cottage was originally built by Silas Patterson in 1853 and today can be found tucked away in a woodland setting in the quaint farming village of Canning.

The view from the two dining rooms and outside patio is one of cultivated flowers intermingled with ferns and other wild greenery growing beneath a canopy of stately elms and maples. The woodland and nearby Habitant River make Bellhill a mecca for songbirds darting among the trees and singing from the branches. The setting is quite idyllic.

The dining rooms are licensed and all food is expertly prepared on the premises. The ladies at Bellhill specialize in using fresh local products and are open for lunch, afternoon tea, summer suppers and Sunday brunch. They will also prepare picnics to take out. A small gift shop featuring works of local artists and household accessories from around the world occupies a small room in the cottage.

Open daily from 11:00 am
Early spring to Dec. 21st
Major credit cards
Proprietors: Wilma Gibson & Elizabeth Rockwell
Main Street
Canning, NS B0P 1H0
(902) 582-7922

THE BLOMIDON INN

Blomidon Inn was built in 1877 by Captain Rufus Burgess, a descendant of the New England Planters. Burgess made his fortune as a ship owner, sailing his fleet from nearby Kingsport on the Bay of Fundy. He directed his captains to bring exotic timber as ballast on their return voyages, and these woods were used to create the magnificent entrance hall and stairway of the inn. Plaster cornices, dados and marble fireplaces were fashioned by Italian craftsmen.

The mansion served as a private residence until the 1940s when it first opened its doors as a hostelry. During the 1950s and 1960s it was a residence for nearby Acadia University, and in 1980 it was restored to its original elegance.

Accommodations are available in 26 beautifully appointed rooms, each with private bath. The inn has two dining rooms; the larger is furnished in fine mahogany Chippendale chairs with a fireplace and a bay window. The smaller, library dining room is a favourite spot for intimate dinners or small groups. Great care is given to the menu which features century-old recipes such as Captain Burgess Rum and Butter Cake or Dutch Appel Taart, both of which are featured in this book.

Popular day trips might include visits to Grand Pré National Historic Park that commemorates the 1755 Expulsion of the Acadians, a hike to the breathtaking cliffs of Cape Split, or just a meander along the tree-lined streets of Wolfville.

Open year round
Major credit cards
Innkeepers: James and Donna Laceby
127 Main Street,
Wolfville, NS,
B0P 1X0
(902) 542-2291

BLUENOSE LODGE

Bluenose Lodge takes its name from the most famous fishing schooner to sail from the port of Lunenburg. Some may even say the *Bluenose* was the most famous sailboat in Canada, as it graces our ten-cent coin. She was built by Smith and Rhuland shipyard and launched in the spring of 1921. Soon to become known as the "Queen of the Grand Bank Schooners", *Bluenose*, with Angus Walters as captain, raced and defeated all her American challengers from 1921 until her last race in 1938.

Bluenose Lodge is situated within walking distance of the Lunenburg waterfront and the town's shops, galleries and many historic buildings. This restored Victorian inn has 9 guests rooms with private baths. Breakfast is included in room rates.

A licensed dining room, specializing in seafood and unique Lunenburg fare, is open for guests and the general public from Mother's Day until late October.

Open year round (November through March, by reservation only)
Major credit cards
Innkeepers: Ron and Grace Swan
10 Falkland Street
Lunenburg, NS,
B0J 2C0
1-800-565-8851,
(902) 634-8851

THE BRAESIDE INN

The Braeside Inn is perched on four acres of hillside lawn overlooking historic Pictou Harbour. Two large dining rooms offer an undisturbed view of the activity of this busy port, while guests sample the fresh Nova Scotia seafood plus an abundance of other offerings.

The town of Pictou is called "the birthplace of New Scotland". The first boatload of Scottish Immigrants arrived on the ship *Hector* in 1773, thus marking the beginning of a wave of Scottish migration which was to have a major impact on the development of the province. It is fitting that today Scottish traditions are still evident. A replica of the *Hector* is under construction; highland games and summer festivals all reflect the Old World heritage.

Conveniently located for day trips, the inn is just a few miles from the Caribou-Wood's Island ferry to Prince Edward Island, and only an hour's drive from Cape Breton Island.

Open year round
Major credit cards
Innkeepers: Anne and Michael Emmett
126 Front Street,
Pictou, NS,
B0K 1H0
(902) 485-5046

THE BRIGHT HOUSE

The Bright House, situated in the town of Sherbrooke, was built as an inn around 1850, but instead became the home of W.D.R. Cameron, the local member of the Nova Scotia Assembly. In 1974, the large frame building with its yellow clapboard siding, finally fulfilled its original intention and was opened to the public as a restaurant.

Hosts Geoffrey Turnbull and Nathalie Blanchet offer their guests country meals with a difference. Traditional fare, such as roast beef with Yorkshire pudding, fresh local seafood, homemade soups and chowders are found on the menu. All dinners begin with marvelous

homemade breads and may be concluded with seasonal fruit desserts. Home baking can be purchased from the owner's bakeshop, located on the property.

Sherbrooke is located on Marine Drive, a pleasant alternate route to Cape Breton, that winds its way past seascapes, sandy beaches and fishing villages. The Bright House is adjacent to Sherbrooke Village, a restored community, where "yesterday meets today." Here, visitors can stroll through history while trying their hand at the tasks their forebears performed.

Season: mid-May to mid-October,
Visa and MasterCard
Restaurateurs: Geoffrey Turnbull and Nathalie Blanchet
P.O. Box 97,
Sherbrooke, NS,
B0J 3C0
(902) 522-2691

CAFÉ CHIANTI

Entering Café Chianti, with its hundreds of wine bottles suspended from the ceiling and its robust atmosphere, is like venturing into a European café. The rooms are cosy and busily noisy; the food is superb and the entertainment on the weekends is first rate.

Chef Thomas Connors offers Northern Italian-Eastern European specialities such as Russian Beef Stroganoff, Chicken Paprikash and a variety of dishes that accent their homemade sausage. The menu also features a varied selection of pasta dishes and fresh local seafood.

Open year round, except Sundays
Major credit cards
Restaurateur: Jan Wicha
5165 South Street,
Halifax, NS
B3J 2A6
(902) 423-7471

CAMPBELL HOUSE

Though he had gained acclaim working at various inns and restaurants throughout the province,

Don Campbell was able to fulfil a lifelong dream with the opening of his own establishment in Chester Basin. At Campbell House you will find the dishes Don is famous for: Caesar Salad, imaginative seafood and meat entrées, plus new delights such as Cream Crowdie, a delectable dessert featured in this book.

Perched on a hill overlooking Mahone Bay, the restaurant is just a few miles from the village of Chester, on Lacey Mines Road. Watch carefully for an unpretentious sign on route 12, north from exit 9 of highway 103. The fine country dining and panoramic view are well worth the search.

Open year round
Major credit cards
Restaurateur: Donald Campbell
321 Lacey Mines Road
Chester Basin, NS,
B0J 1K0
(902) 275-5655

CANDLERIGGS

Located in the scenic village of Indian Harbour, next to Peggy's Cove, this fine establishment has been pleasing patrons since 1973.

The dining room at Candleriggs specializes in using fresh local seafood, meat and produce. Owner Jean Cochrane calls upon her own heritage to serve guests traditional Scottish dishes such as Forfar Bridie, Haddock Braemar, Haggis and Steak and Kidney Pie. Scottish afternoon tea is served, and during the summer months, a traditional Ayrshire breakfast.

The adjacent craftshop has an acclaimed reputation for its quality Canadian art and handcrafts, including an impressive display of designer class pottery, pewter and handblown art glass.

Open daily (mid-January to mid-March, weekends only)
Major credit cards
Restaurateur: Jean Cochrane
Indian Harbour,
Halifax Co., NS,
B0J 3J0
(902) 823-2722

THE CAPTAIN'S HOUSE

The Captain's House inn, dining room and lounge is situated on the back harbour of Chester. Originally known as Shoreham, this 1822 structure was built on Lot No.1 by New Englander Reverend John Secombe. The view from the dining room and outdoor patio of this Georgian inn offers guests a spectacular view of Mahone Bay and some of its 365 islands, one to explore each day of the year.

Nine guest rooms, each with private bath, are located in the inn amid period furnishings and a unique art collection. As well, the inn's private dock can accommodate craft up to 40 feet in length.

Open year round
Major credit cards
Innkeepers: Nicki Butler and Jane McLoughlin
129 Central Street
Chester, NS,
B0J 1J0
(902) 275-3501

CHEZ LA VIGNE

Chez La Vigne (The Grapevine Café) is located in the picturesque university town of Wolfville. Situated at the eastern end of the Annapolis Valley, Wolfville looks out toward Cape Blomidon over miles of dykelands that run down to the shore of the Minas Basin.

Alex Clavel, the owner-operator of Chez La Vigne, brings to your table his knowledge and expertise as an internationally renowned chef. In 1989 he was chosen Chef of the Year by his peers at the Canadian Federation of Chefs de Cuisine.

For this cookbook, Chef Clavel created special recipes that he feels are an expression of Bay of Fundy–Annapolis Valley cuisine, and which utilize the fine products of this area.

Seafood and artful meal presentations are the specialities at Chez La Vigne. Alex Clavel grows his own herbs and uses the freshest products available.

Open year round 10:00 a.m.-10:00 p.m. Winter 10 a.m.-9 p.m.
Visa and MasterCard
Restaurateur: Alex Clavel
17 Front Street
Wolfville, NS,
B0P 1X0
(902) 542-5077

THE COBEQUID INN

This small inn is located in Selma on Nova Scotia's Cobequid Bay. Dating back to 1828, this old farmhouse and former post office was transformed to its present state in the 1970s. The inn offers 3 rooms with 2 shared baths and includes full breakfast, at guest's convenience. Guests may enjoy hiking trails, bicycles, lawn games and an above-ground pool.

A licensed dining room, serving dinner from 5 to 9 p.m. is open to the general public and features fresh seafood and meats served with seasonal vegetables from the inn's garden.

This area was one of many in the province well known for its wooden sailing vessels. At the

W.D. Lawrence Museum, located nearby, visitors can view memorabilia of this exciting era. Across the road from the museum, the largest sailing vessel built in Canada was launched in 1874. Also near the inn is Burntcoat Head which boasts the highest tides in the world, with a vertical distance of 54 feet between high and low tide.

Season: May through October (off-season by reservation)
Visa and MasterCard
Innkeepers: Jim and Nancy Cleveland
RR#1,
Maitland, NS,
B0N 1T0
(902) 261-2841

THE COMPASS ROSE INN

The Compass Rose Inn is located one block from the harbourfront in the historic seaport of Lunenburg. This provincial heritage property was built in 1825 and is a classic example of Georgian architecture.

Owned and operated by Suzanne and Rodger Pike, the inn offers guests an intimate lounge, gift shop, outdoor garden patio and rooms with private bath, sitting area and complimentary tea and coffee. The Pikes also manage the Lion Inn, a bed and breakfast, located two blocks away at 33 Cornwallis Street.

The restaurant at the Compass Rose specializes in fine cuisine and features traditional German-style Lunenburg dishes and fresh seafood.

Season: mid-February to December (breakfast, lunch and dinner)
Major credit cards
Innkeepers: Rodger and Suzanne Pike
15 King Street
Lunenburg, NS,
B0J 2C0
(902) 634-8509

COOPER'S INN AND RESTAURANT

Cooper's Inn, located in Shelburne on Nova Scotia's South Shore, was built in 1785 by George Gracie, a blind Loyalist merchant. Over the centuries it has been home to shipbuilders, mariners, merchants, and coopers (barrel makers). This inn, authentically restored by owners Cynthia and Gary Hynes, is a Registered Nova Scotia Heritage Property.

The inn offers 5 guestrooms, 3 in the main building and 2 in the adjoining cooperage, all with private baths and wonderful harbour views. Cooper's Inn offers full dining facilities featuring regional cuisine and fresh local produce. The atmosphere is relaxed yet with expert service that ensures a comfortable ambience so guests may linger over coffee and conversation.

Season: April through October
Visa, MasterCard and American Express
Innkeepers: Gary and Cynthia Hynes
Dock Street and Mason Lane
Shelburne, NS,
B0T 1W0
(902) 875-4656

DA MAURIZIO DINING ROOM

Da Maurizio's dining room occupies the lower level of a building which once which housed Alexander Keith's brewery. Known affectionately by locals as "the brewery", the area is located on the busy harbour-front.

Amid a setting of crisp linens, fine china and profuse greenery, Da Maurizio's is open for evening dining only. The menu is varied and extensive, featuring continental cuisine. Patrons apreciate the careful attention given by the chefs to the inclusion of fresh Atlantic seafood and produce. At this restaurant you can expect a wide range of appealing appetizers, salads, entrees and delectable desserts.

Open year round
Mondays through Saturdays, 5:00 pm - 10:00 pm
Major credit cards
1496 Lower Water Street
Halifax, NS, B3J 1R9
(902) 423-0859

DUNCREIGAN COUNTRY INN OF MABOU

Mabou would definitely have been a Scottish Highlander's idea of heaven in the New World. This little village on Cape Breton's Ceilidh Trail abounds with natural beauty and is steeped in Gaelic culture and tradition. The newly built Duncreigan Country Inn is situated among trees on the edge of Mabou's inner harbour. It features four bright and airy guestrooms, all with private bath and bowed windows that overlook either the saltwater estuary or the inn's gardens.

Breakfast and dinner are served at Duncreigan's licensed harbour front dining room

to guests and the general public. Cocktails and afternoon tea are served in the parlour. Using only the finest fresh products available, the owners have successfully married newer health-conscious trends with traditional Cape Breton fare.

Open year round
Visa and MasterCard
Innkeepers: Eleanor and Charles Mullendore
P.O. Box 59,
Mabou, Cape Breton, NS,
B0E 1X0
(902) 945-2207

THE GALLEY

The Galley restaurant is part of the South Shore Marine complex, home to 325 yachts at Marriott's Cove in Mahone Bay.

The nautical decor of this fine restaurant carries over to the adjacent Tic-O-Fog Lounge, and aptly named giftshop, the Loft, where you can find unique marine items and charts. In addition, South Shore Marine provides special meeting facilities and a boardroom with seating for 18.

The Galley features homemade soups and chowders, summer salads, the freshest of seafoods and sumptuous desserts. Whether you arrive by land or by sea, the Galley promises the splendour of an Atlantic sunset for your personal reflection and enjoyment.

Season: March through
December
Major credit cards
Manager: Janet Eisenhauer
Marriott's Cove, Box 316
Chester, NS,
B0J 1J0
(902) 275-4700

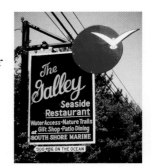

THE GARRISON HOUSE INN

Garrison House Inn is just one of many restored historic properties you will find as you stroll the tranquil streets of Annapolis Royal. The town, Canada's oldest permanent settlement was founded, by the French, under Samuel de Champlain in 1605. After scenes of conflict

the dramatic whiteness of the buildings set against a background of dark green forest and blue sky. The complex was designed so that MacLellan's Brook could meander between and around the buildings. The structures are constructed with post and beam framing and stone walls in traditional Scottish style.

Set on 200 acres, Glenora Inn and Distillery, is comprised of an inn with 9 guestrooms, licensed dining room and lounge, gift shop, and the only single malt whisky distillery in North America. The distillery has a production capacity of 600,000 litres of whisky, the Gaelic "Uisge Beatha" or "Water of Life"; as well, Glenora blends and bottles white and dark rum. Conducted tours are available to guests and the public.

The dining room is open for breakfast, lunch, afternoon "high tea" and dinner. The restaurant features fine country cuisine with a touch of Scottish fare, such as Steak and Kidney Pie and Cranachan.

Season: May through October (other times by appointment)
Visa, MasterCard, American Express
Innkeeper: Lauchie Maclean
P.O. Box 181, RR#4 Mabou
Cape Breton, NS,
B0E 1X0
(902) 258-2662

between Britain and France in the seventeenth century, the town finally passed to the British in 1710 and became the capital of Nova Scotia until 1749. Annapolis Royal and environs offer visitors live theatre, museums, golf, picturesque touring and the Annapolis Royal Historic Gardens, one of Canada's finest theme gardens.

The inn itself was originally built in 1854 as the Temperance Hotel. It currently offers 7 guest rooms, most with private bath. Well known for its fine food, the inn's intimate licensed dining room offers the public breakfast, lunch, dinner and during the high season, English Cream Teas.

Season: May through November (weekends until Christmas)
Visa, MasterCard, American Express
Innkeeper: Patrick Redgrave
350 St. George Street
Annapolis Royal, NS, B0S 1A0
(902) 532-5750

GLENORA INN AND DISTILLERY

This unique establishment is located at Glenville on the Ceilidh Trail in the heart of the Cape Breton highlands. The first thing one notices is

Louisbourg, Miner's Museum and Cabot Trail are all less than an hour's drive.

Season: April to October 30th
Visa and MasterCard
Innkeepers: Clifford Matthews and Ken Tutty
139 Shore Road
Sydney Mines, NS,
B1V 1A6
(902) 544-1050

GOWRIE HOUSE COUNTRY INN

Gowrie House was built for a Mr. Archibald, agent general of the General Mining Association, in 1830. His wife, suffering from homesickness, named the new house after her home, Blair Gowrie, in their native Scotland. Overcoming their initial melancholy, the Archibalds became permanent Canadian residents and the home remained in the family until purchased in 1975 by its current owner Clifford Matthews.

Gowrie House has 6 guestrooms in the main inn and 4 suites in the Garden House. All rooms are furnished with antiques and decorated to enhance a feeling of comfortable elegance. The grounds are beautifully maintained and the gardens invite you to sit and enjoy the surroundings. A full breakfast is included with lodging.

Dinner is served to guests and the general public at one sitting, with advance reservation. The inn is known for its fine dining and uses only the fresh produce from the fields, waters and gardens of Nova Scotia.

Gowrie House is a convenient starting point for touring Cape Breton and minutes away from the Newfoundland ferry terminal. The Alexander Graham Bell Museum, Fortress

HADDON HALL INN

The view from the dining room and grounds of Haddon Hall Inn is quite simply magnificent. The property was built in 1905 by Vernon Woolrich as a summer residence and named after his wife's family home in England. It remained in private hands until 1994 when it was transformed into a luxury 4-star inn and restaurant.

This impressive establishment occupies 90 acres of a prominent hill in the seaside vacation village of Chester. Seagulls call overhead as, below you, the sun shines on scores of islands dotted about the blue waters of Mahone Bay.

Guests may choose from luxurious rooms in the main house or quaint cottages and lodges throughout the grounds of the estate. Patrons receive a complimentary continental breakfast and use of the tennis court, heated outdoor pool and boat shuttle to the inn's private island with white sand beach.

The licensed dining room is open to the public for lunch, dinner and Sunday brunch.

Open year round
Major credit cards
Manager: Cynthia O'Connell
67 Haddon Hill Road
Chester, NS
B0J 1J0
(902) 275-3577 or 275-3578

HALLIBURTON HOUSE INN

This small elegant hotel is situated on a quiet street in downtown Halifax, located a few blocks from the waterfront and the business core of the capital city. Shops, museums and parks are just a short walk from the front door.

Built between 1809 and 1860, this stone and brick building was once the home of Sir Brenton Halliburton, the first chief justice of the Supreme Court of Nova Scotia. The inn incorporates three registered heritage townhouses, each impeccably restored to its former elegance and decorated appropriately in period antiques.

On the menu of the Halliburton House you will find fresh Atlantic seafood as well as wild game entrées, such as pheasant and buffalo steak. The restaurant is open for lunch and dinner: during summer months guests can enjoy lunch in the outdoor garden cafe.

Open year round (reservations suggested for dinner)
Major credit cards
Innkeeper: Robert Pretty
5184 Morris St.,
Halifax, NS, B3J 1B3
(902) 420-0658

THE INNLET CAFÉ

Mahone Bay is a small town built on the edge of the sea. Three churches stand side-by-side at the head of the harbour, their colorful spires serving as beacons to the many fishermen of the area. Today, the quiet town abounds in the arts. There is an antique centre, pottery and pewter

studios, art gallery and many fine craft shops.

It is easy to understand why the Innlet Café is the dining focal point of visits to the area. Jack and Katherine Sorenson specialize in serving seafoods, chowders, home baked goods and delectable desserts in their dining room or on their summer terrace.

Open year round for lunch and dinner
Major credit cards
Restauranteurs: Jack and Katherine Sorenson
R R#2 Keddy's Landing
Mahone Bay, NS, B0J 2E0
(902) 624-6363

INN-ON-THE-LAKE

Conveniently located 10 minutes from the Halifax International Airport, en route to Halifax-Dartmouth, this small hotel is set on five acres of parkland at the edge of beautiful Lake Thomas.

Guests are invited to use the free shuttlebus service to the airport, as well as enjoy the inn's amenities, such as tennis, shuffle board, jogging paths, white sand beach, heated pool, wind surfers, paddleboats and much more.

Award-winning chef Roland Glauser presents a menu following a seasonal theme, using the best local ingredients and produce. Meals are served in the main dining room, in Oliver's Pub, on the terrace or by the gazebo bar in the park. Breakfast, lunch and dinner are served daily from 7 a.m.

Open year round
Major credit cards
Innkeepers: Ronald and Susan Nelson
P. O. Box 29,
Waverley, NS, B0N 2S0
(902) 861-3480

INVERARY INN RESORT

Inverary Inn Resort, located on the shores of the Bras d'Or Lakes, in the village of Baddeck, is a one-stop vacation centre for people of all ages and interests. The inn offers guests tennis, indoor and outdoor pools, fitness centre, sauna, lawn games and water related activities including canoeing and boat cruises. Winter activities include sleigh rides, nordic skiing and snowmobiling.

The recent addition of a first-class convention centre has made Inverary a likely choice for group functions including the 1993 Canadian Premier's Conference hosted by the Province of Nova Scotia. A variety of accommodations are available, such as, cosy pine-panelled cottages, hotel and motel units and antique furnished guest rooms in the lodge. The main dining room serves fine country cuisine with such local specialties as Scottish oatcakes, smoked salmon and bannock. The casual Fish House Restaurant on the waterfront is open during the summer months.

Baddeck is a major tourist destination for yachtsmen and highway travellers. Of note is the Alexander Graham Bell Museum, which houses much of the inventor's memorabilia and inventions. The museum looks across the bay to Beinn Breagh, summer home of the inventor for the last 37 years of his life. His descendants still own and vacation on the site.

Season: May through November
Major credit cards
Innkeeper: Scott MacAulay
PO Box 190, Baddeck, NS
B0E 1B0
(902) 295-3500

KELTIC LODGE

In the late 1800s, Henry Corson of Akron, Ohio, exclaimed, "My dear, that is the place!" He was referring to a spectacular, surf tossed finger of land jutting out into the ocean — what the locals called Middle Head. Seeking a healthier environment for Mrs. Corson, who had tuberculosis, the Corsons purchased Middle Head. They built a large log home, planted orchards and established a thriving dairy farm.

Today, the homestead has been replaced by Keltic's cosy cottages and large white lodge and the grazing fields transformed into a challenging golf course. But do not fear, the clear unpolluted air and spectacular vista of ocean and mountains is still there just as Henry Corson discovered it.

Keltic Lodge is one of Nova Scotia's oldest

and best resort hotels. Operated by the Province of Nova Scotia, it offers guests elegant accommodation and fine dining — in fact, one of the most consistent and imaginative dining rooms in the region. No visitor to Cape Breton should miss it. The dining room is open to both guests and the public for breakfast, lunch and dinner (dinner dress code). The resort features an ocean beach, outdoor pool, lawn games, nature trails, tennis courts, and gift shop. Special romance, golf, whale watching and Cabot Trail touring packages are available.

Season: June to October
(Ski season: January to March)
Major credit cards
Manager: Alexander MacClure
Middle Head Peninsula,
Ingonish Beach, NS,
B0C 1L0
(902) 285-2880

La Perla

La Perla is an intimate restaurant located in the heart of downtown Dartmouth, and only a minute's walk from the ferry linking the sister city of Halifax. A window table ensures a view of the harbour and waterfront!

Noted for its northern Italian cuisine, the dining room features a variety of dishes not often found elsewhere in the metro area. Careful preparation using only the freshest of ingredients ensure a delightful meal. You can expect to find Risotto, Zuppa di Pesce and Gnocchi, plus a variety of seafood, pasta and veal dishes.

Open daily for dinner;
Monday to Friday for lunch
Major credit cards
Restaurateur: Pearl MacDougal
71 Alderney Drive,
Dartmouth, NS,
B2Y 2N7
(902) 469-3241

LISCOMBE LODGE

Liscombe Lodge, one of Nova Scotia's finest resorts and dining rooms, is nestled among the trees at the edge of a swiftly flowing river on Nova Scotia's eastern shore. Owned by the provincial government which also owns the equally fine Digby Pines and Keltic Lodge, Liscombe offers guests a complete vacation retreat. Accommodation ranges from chalets that are within sight and sound of rushing rapids, to European-style cottages and large rooms in the lodge, all with private balcony.

The resort offers guests an ambience of relaxation with its marina, boat and canoe

rentals, tennis courts, playground, enclosed pool, fitness spa and hiking trails. Staff will arrange deep-sea fishing charters as well as guides for Atlantic salmon angling.

The chefs at Liscombe Lodge have a well-earned reputation for their fine renditions of local dishes such as planked salmon, seafood chowders and desserts that utilize seasonal fruits and berries.

The informal but elegant verandah-styled licensed dining room has a splendid view over the river and is open to the public for breakfast, lunch and dinner.

Season: June through October
Major credit cards
Manager: David M. Evans
Liscomb Mills, NS
B0J 2A0
(902) 779-2307

MacAskill's Restaurant

MacAskill's Restaurant takes its name from giant Angus MacAskill, a famous figure in Nova Scotia

history. Angus was born in Scotland but moved to Cape Breton in 1825 at the age of three. This gentle man grew to a height of 7 feet 9 inches and became famous for his feats of strength. Upon hearing stories of his amazing abilities, Queen Victoria invited him to Windsor Castle where she presented him with two gold rings and proclaimed him the "tallest, stoutest, strongest man that ever entered the place."

MacAskill's is located in the ferry terminal on the waterfront in downtown Dartmouth. From the restaurant's dining room and patio, patrons are treated to a panoramic view of harbour activities and the Halifax shoreline. The restaurant offers guests a varied menu highlighted with seafood specialities.

Open daily dinner, lunch Monday to Friday
Major credit cards
Manager: Sandy Chaisson
88 Adlerney Drive,
P. O. Box 976
Dartmouth, NS
B2Y 3Z6
(902) 466-3100

IL MERCATO RISTORANTE

Il Mercato is located on Spring Garden Road, one Halifax' busiest pedestrian districts. This small Italian-styled bistro with its red tiled floors, fresco painted walls and greenery is popular with the lunch and dinner crowd.

The meal begins when your server introduces you to the tradition of dipping your pannini (Italian bread) in balsamic vinegar and olive oil. The menu features authentic Mediterranean-style fare offering a variety of appetizers, soups, salads, pastas, pizzas and sandwiches. For heartier dining the chef prepares several seafood and meat entrees. End your meal with one of Il Mercato's gelatos or delicious desserts.

Open Monday to Saturday, 11am to 11pm
No reservations
Take-out menu available
Manager: Merrill Jones
5475 Spring Garden Road
Halifax, NS, B3J 3T2
(902) 422-2866

MILFORD HOUSE

Milford House is a nature lovers' retreat set amid the tranquil woods and rippling waters of southern Nova Scotia. Constructed in the 1860s by Abraham Thomas as a "halfway house for travellers," the inn remained in the Thomas family until 1969. At that time, ownership transferred to a group of former guests who were determined to operate Milford House in its previous manner and to preserve its 600 acres of woodland.

Twenty-seven cottages of various sizes, all with fireplaces, verandas and private docks are strung along the shores of two lakes. They are within walking distance of the main lodge, where wholesome country breakfasts and dinners are served to guests, under the Modified American Plan.

Guests may enjoy the inn's tennis courts, children's play area, lawn games, fishing, walking

trails, lake swimming, canoeing, refreshing sunrises and relaxing sunsets.

Season: June 15 to September 15 (2 winterized cottages available off-season)
Visa
Manager: Maggie Nickerson
RR #4 P. O. Box 521
Annapolis Royal, NS
B0S 1A0
(902) 532-2617

THE MOUNTAIN GAP INN AND RESORT

Mountain Gap is a large complex offering all the amenities for a complete vacation. Nearing a century of service to the public, the resort has a beach, a pool, tennis and shuffleboard courts, outdoor chess, plus 45 acres of gardens and natural woodlands to roam.

The atmosphere is relaxed at Mountain Gap, and the fireplaced diningroom overlooking the sea offers a variety of fresh Nova Scotian seafood and traditional dishes, to guests and the public. Accommodations are available in over 100 rooms, including cottages and family units.

Nearby attractions include the provincial theme and wildlife parks, golf, and whale watching tours. Arrangements can be made at the inn to partake in any of these local activities.

Season: mid-May through mid-October
Major credit cards
Innkeeper: Ann Goddard
P. O. Box 504
Digby, NS
B0V 1C0
toll free 1-800-565-5020

NEMO'S RESTAURANT

The thick stone walls and historic setting of Nemo's makes this intimate restaurant an special place to dine.

Located on Hollis Street, the dining room is a short stroll from the major hotels, boutiques and shops which line the downtown Halifax streets.

Specialities include offerings from various cuisines, including Provençale and northern Italian. Careful presentation and a masterful use of herbs and spices enhances, but never overwhelms their dishes. Look for innovative soups and appetizers, local seafoods such as swordfish and scallops, veal and lamb entrées, plus a variety of great desserts.

Open daily for dinner; Monday to Saturday for lunch
Major credit cards
Restaurateur: Brian Trainor
1865 Hollis Street
Halifax, NS
B3J 1W5
(902) 425-6738

THE NORMAWAY INN

Salmon anglers and travellers have been frequenting the Normaway Inn in the beautiful Margaree Valley of the Cape Breton Highlands since 1928. A drive down the tree-lined lane of this 250-acre resort will guarantee you instant immersion in the traditions and hospitality of the region.

Whether your interest is angling on one of North America's finest salmon and trout rivers, or exploring the beauties of nature through photography, hiking or touring, the Margaree will satisfy your desires. The Normaway also offers guests tennis, a recreation barn, lawn games, walking trails and weekly live entertainment in the true Cape Breton Gaelic tradition. A short drive down the valley will find you on the Gulf of St. Lawrence with its expansive white beaches and deep-sea fishing.

The inn offers 9 bedrooms with a common living room and library as well as 19 one and two-bedroom cabins. The dining room is open to guests and the general public and serves gourmet country cooking specializing in local meats, seafood and produce from the inn's garden.

Season: mid-June to mid-October
MasterCard and Visa
Innkeeper: David MacDonald
Egypt Road,
Margaree Valley, NS
B0E 2C0
(902) 248-2987 or 1-800-565-9463 toll free

THE PALLISER

The Palliser complex sits on land settled by British pioneers in 1760 — the first English speaking people to arrive in the area. Today, the pastoral setting is an ideal spot for viewing the Bay of Fundy tidal bore. This natural phenomenon created by the unique geography of the bay permits a bore of water to rush up-river, crashing against the banks and rocks to fill a broad channel in 20 minutes. This event occurs twice daily, and staff at the Palliser will gladly indicate the best times and sites for viewing.

The restaurant at the Palliser reflects Nova Scotian hospitality at its very best. Four generations of the Bruce family have been providing home-style meals in their charming

dining room, and it is understandable why their Lobster Feed has become a perennial favourite. In addition to the notable crustacean, look for a menu featuring homemade soups, seafood, chicken, beef or lamb entrées and an array of wonderful desserts.

The Palliser offers 42 motel units, an extensive gift shop and restaurant. Since Truro is considered the "crossroads" of Atlantic Canada, it is an ideal starting point for a Maritime vacation.

Season: May through November
Major credit cards
Innkeepers: Keltie and Allan Bruce
P. O. Box 821
Truro, NS
B2N 5G6
(902) 893-8951

THE PINES RESORT HOTEL

Originally operated as one of the Canadian Pacific Railway's luxury destination resorts, "The Pines" is currently operated by the Province of Nova Scotia. This elegant hotel is located on a pine covered hill overlooking the beautiful Annapolis Basin, a short distance from the St. John–Digby ferry terminal. The Norman-style main hotel contains 83 tastefully decorated rooms and suites, while 30 cottages with living rooms and stone fireplaces, are located nearby.

Features of the hotel include fitness centre, outdoor heated pool, tennis courts, championship golf course, lawn games, walking trails, gift shop and a director of guest services. Breakfast, lunch and dinner are served in the hotel's Annapolis Room. The chefs at the resort specialize in artfully presented, fine continental cuisine.

Season: Late May to mid October
Major credit cards
Manager: Maurice G. Thiebaut
Shore Road, P. O. Box 70
Digby, NS
B0V 1A0
toll-free 1-800-667-4637

THE PLANTERS' BARRACKS

In 1760 the Planters came to Starr's Point, Nova Scotia from New England to occupy the rich dyked farmland left unattended after the expulsion of the Acadians. In 1778 the British Army built Fort Hughes to protect the settlement. Later, the building served as a custom's house for the port of Cornwallis. Planters' Barracks is the oldest authentically restored inn in the province.

The "barracks", with its 9 guest rooms offers traditional hospitality in a rural setting. Guests may play tennis, stroll in the gardens or relax in one of the inn's keeping rooms. Guests and the public may enjoy lunch or afternoon tea in the adjacent Acaciacroft Tea Room. Dinner is available to guests with advance arrangement.

Inn Open Year-Round, Tea Room May through October
Major Credit Cards
Innkeepers: Jennie Sheito with Ted & Grace Fraser
1464-1468 Starrs Point Road
Port Williams, NS B0P 1T0
(902) 542-7879 or 1-800-661-4442

SALMON RIVER HOUSE COUNTRY INN

The Salmon River House Country Inn is situated on the edge of the Salmon River where it meets the ocean at the Head of Jeddore. It is nestled at the base of a steep, forested hill and adjacent to the Marine Drive on Nova Scotia's Eastern Shore.

The inn features 6 guest rooms, all with private bath or shower including a wheelchair accessible family suite. The inn offers guests relaxation in their library and sun room, as well as onsite hiking, fishing, hunting and boating. A licensed dining room is open for guests and the general public for breakfast, lunch and dinner.

Nearby you will find miles of white sand beaches for bathing and beachcombing, coves and bays for birdwatching and photographing and the provincial government's Fisherman's Life Museum depicting the life of an inshore fisherman's family at the turn of the century.

Season: April through December (January to March by appointment)
Visa, MasterCard
Innkeepers: Norma and Adrian Blanchette
Salmon River Bridge
RR# 2 Head of Jeddore, NS, B0J 1P0
(902) 889-3353

SCANWAY RESTAURANT

Enjoy a charming Scandivanian dining experience in the heart of downtown Halifax at Scanway Restaurant. Owner Unni Simemsen shares her culture by preparing memorable dishes from her homeland.

While the luncheon menu features gourmet open-faced sandwiches, and cool, crisp salads accented with herbs, the dinner menu includes pepper steak, chicken and seafood selections. But the *pièce de résistance* of Scanway is their outstanding array of delectable desserts!

Open 11:30am - 10:00 pm, Monday through Saturday
Major credit cards
Restaurateur: Unni Simemsen
1569 Dresden Row
Halifax, NS
B3J 2K4
(902) 422-3733

THE SILVER SPOON

The Silver Spoon Restaurant and Silver Spoon Desserts are located in a handsome newly renovated house amid the hotel and banking district in downtown Halifax.

A ground floor café specializes in lighter meals and desserts, for which they have become famous. Upstairs in the more formal dining room, owner Deanna Silver offers a varied, imaginative and often-changing menu which includes contemporary dishes and makes full use of locally available fresh produce and seafood.

Open daily for lunch and dinner
Major credit cards
Restaurateur: Deanna Silver
1813 Granville Street
Halifax, NS, B3J 1X8
(902) 422-1519

TATTINGSTONE INN

This elegant English-style country inn is decorated with eighteenth-century antiques, yet it offers today's guests all the modern comforts. A music room with grand piano, well-stocked library, tennis court, outdoor heated pool, steam room and beautiful gardens are available for guests' use.

Located in the small university town of Wolfville, visitors will find this a central location for a variety of activities — touring, photography, birdwatching, or browsing for arts and crafts.

The dining room at Tattingstone Inn is open for breakfast to guests and open to the general public for afternoon tea and dinner. Reservations are recommended.

Open year round
Major credit cards
Innkeeper: Betsey Harwood
434 Main Street,
P. O. Box 98,
Wolfville, NS
B0P 1X0
(902) 542-7696

UPPER DECK WATERFRONT FISHERY AND GRILL

This fine restaurant is located in the Privateers' Warehouse of Historic Properties on the Halifax waterfront. Built by Enos Collins, this 200-year old structure has been home to many things — from the booty of the privateers of old to the present-day restaurant. The dining room has retained the nautical flavour of its origins with its heavy beams and ship models, including the famed Nova Scotian schooner *Bluenose*.

Since its conception in 1975, the Upper Deck Waterfront Fishery and Grill has gained a reputation for impeccably prepared seafood as well as delectable desserts.

Open daily for dinner
Major credit cards
Manager: Allan Johnston
Privateer's Warehouse
Historic Properties
Halifax, NS
B3J 2X1
(902) 422-1289

VICTORIA'S HISTORIC INN

Residents of the Wolfville area are indeed fortunate to have an unprecedented number of fine inns and eateries; quite possibly the greatest concentration of excellent cuisine in Atlantic Canada. Victoria's Historic Inn is a well deserved part of this reputation. The Cryan family graciously welcome guests to their inn erected in 1880 by the prosperous apple merchant W.H. Chase.

The structure was built in true Victorian manner and has been restored to its original style complete with gingerbread decorated verandas, ornamental eaves and sheltered entries. The interior woodwork and stained-glass windows are a tribute to the fine craftsmanship of this era. Of particular architectural interest are six fireplaces, each with uniquely different mantels of fruitwood, oak or marble.

Victoria's Historic Inn features 8 guest rooms and a 2 bedroom suite decorated in period Victorian fashion in the main building, as well as 6 intimate rooms in the recently refurbished coach house. Excellent cuisine specializing in fresh seafood is featured in the licensed dining room. Open year round for breakfast, May 1st to January 1st for dinner; reservations recommended. Winter dinners are available with weekend packages.

Open year round
Major credit cards
Innkeepers: Urbain & Carol Cryan
416 Main Street
PO Box 308 Wolfville, NS, B0P 1X0
(902) 542-5744

THE WALKER INN

The Walker Inn is located in Pictou, a town known as the "birthplace of New Scotland." This centrally located inn occupies the upper three floors of a four-storey property that dates from 1865. Owners Felix and Theresa Walker, young expatriates of Switzerland, bring an enthusiastic European flair to their establishment. Ten guest rooms are available, all with private bath, and many with a view of the harbour. Buffet continental breakfast is served to guests.

The inn also operates a licensed dining room, featuring three-course, continental cuisine dinners by reservation.

Open year round
Visa, American Express and MasterCard
Innkeepers: Felix and Theresa Walker
34 Coleraine Street
Pictou, NS, B0K 1H0
(902) 485-1433

WHITE POINT BEACH LODGE RESORT

The ambience surrounding White Point Beach Lodge is magical whether the sun shines on the sparkling surf or the fog rolls in. This resort is located on its own white sand crescent beach and offers guests accommodations in lodge-style rooms or woodland and ocean front cottages.

This is a nature lover's haven with woodland, shoreline and ocean at your beck and call. Breath in the ocean air and commune with the environment. Guests may enjoy on site tennis, golf, boating activities, children's playground, indoor and outdoor pools and fitness centre. Conference facilities are available and the licensed dining room is open to guests and the public for breakfast, lunch and dinner.

Open year round
Major credit cards
Manager: Doug Fawthrop
Box 9000, Liverpool, NS B0T 1G0
Hwy #103 exit 20A or 21 to Rt. 3
(902) 354-2711 NS & PEI 1-800-665-4863
Other 1-800-565-5068

THE WHITMAN INN

Innkeepers Nancy and Bruce Gurnham honeymooned in Nova Scotia at Kejimkujik National Park some years ago. They were so enamoured with the area that they changed their careers and bought an old home at Caledonia, Queens County, near their beloved "Keji". Today this beautiful country inn offers guests a blend of peace and tranquility, outdoor activity and fine food.

Whitman Inn is a turn-of-the-century homestead, fully restored with original furnishings. Breakfast is served to house guests and candlelit dinners to guests and the public by reservation only; arrangements can also be made for hearty picnic baskets to take on excursions.

The inn features an indoor pool and sauna. Special park-related canoeing, cross-country skiing and bicycling packages can be arranged.

Open year round
Major credit cards
Innkeepers: Bruce and Nancy Gurnham
RR #2 Caledonia, NS, B0T 1B0
(902) 682-2226

PRINCE EDWARD ISLAND

There is something magical about Prince Edward Island. The houses are painted a white that is brighter than sunlight, and the colour of the green grass and red soil is a hue deeper than any found elsewhere in Canada. Here, you can expect excellent fresh food and genuine warm hospitality.

DALVAY-BY-THE-SEA

Built by Alexander MacDonald at the end of the last century, Dalvay is one of the Maritime's most elegant country inns. Warm wood panelling, a giant sandstone fireplace and rooms filled with antiques await guests, while the warm waters and sweeping dunes of Brackley Beach National Park are just a stone's throw away. Tennis courts, croquet greens, golf, bike trails and miles of spectacular beaches are but a few of the amenities at Dalvay.

The elegant dining room specializes in local seafood, the freshest produce and the most delectable desserts.

Season: June through September
Major credit cards
Innkeeper: David Thompson
Box 8,
Little York, PEI
C0A 1P0
(902) 672-2048

Season: Late May to mid-October
Visa and MasterCard
Innkeeper: David Wilmer
Bay Fortune
R R #4 Souris, PEI
C0A 2B0
(902) 687-3745

THE INN AT BAY FORTUNE

The inn is situated on 46 acres of land that faces Bay Fortune as it opens out to the Northumberland Strait, 8 miles from the Magdalen Islands' ferry in Souris and 45 miles from Charlottetown, the Island's capital.

The lodge was built in 1910 as a summer hideaway by playwright Elmer Harris, author of the 1940s Broadway hit *Johnny Belinda*. The inn features 11 spacious suites, each with a view of

the sea and a romantic sitting area with a fireplace. A four-storey tower includes a common room observatory and telescope.

Chef Michael Smith calls Prince Edward Island "a chef's paradise." He prepares local produce, giving the menu an overall contemporary focus. The recipes featured in this book are signature Island dishes for which the inn has become famous.

THE LOYALIST COUNTRY INN

Fittingly located overlooking the waterfront in the heart of downtown Summerside, the Loyalist Country Inn offers elegant, traditional amenities in the style of a New England country inn.

Summerside, on the southwestern side of the island, was once home to a lucrative fox-raising industry and shipbuilding. Today, a drive up the residential streets of town will take you back to the time when shipbuilders and fox breeders were the Island's high society. Some of the elegant homes built over 100 years ago have been dubbed "fox houses", a term which refers to fortunes made and lost in the silver fox industry. Local attractions include museums, golf courses and the endless miles of beaches.

Open year round
Major credit cards
Manager: JoAnne Schurman
195 Harbour Drive
Summerside, PEI
C1N 5R1
(902) 436-3333

The Matthew House Inn

THE MATTHEW HOUSE INN

The Matthew House, former home of Uriah Matthew, a late nineteenth-century entrepreneur, charmingly offers Victorian ambience in Souris. Located on Breakwater Street, this elegant hideaway features hearty breakfasts for guests and gourmet lunches or candlelight dinners by arrangement. The Matthew House offers 8 guest rooms, each with private bath.

Area activities include birdwatching for shorebirds, herons, kingfishers and osprey. Walk along miles of white sand beaches or visit East Point lighthouse where you can watch the churning tides of the Northumberland Strait meet the Gulf of St. Lawrence — a vista unsurpassed in the Maritimes.

Season: June through October 15th
Major credit cards
Innkeepers: Linda Anderson and Emma Cappelluzzo
15 Breakwater Street
Souris, PEI
C0A 2B0
(902) 687-3461

McCRADY'S GREEN ACRES

Nestled in a quiet corner in Cornwall, just 10 minutes from downtown Charlottetown, is McCrady's Green Acres Motel and Restaurant. This quiet country setting borders the scenic West River.

While host and European Master Chef David Bradshaw specializes in English favourites, a broad variety of European and Canadian dishes are also served. McCrady's central location

makes it an ideal starting point for a cycling vacation and day-trips to Charlottetown.

Season: mid-June to mid-September
Major credit cards
Innkeepers: David and Yvonne Bradshaw
RR#2
Cornwall, PEI
C0A 1H0
(902) 566-4938

SHAW'S HOTEL

When Great Grandfather Shaw opened an inn on the family's pioneer farm in 1860, he wanted to provide relaxing country lodging for visitors to the Island. A fourth generation of the Shaw family continue this tradition today.

Decorated in traditional Island style, the property encompasses the original farmhouse, 17 cottages and a lodge. Famed Brackley Beach, with its pink sand and windswept dunes, is only a five-minute walk through a shaded lane from the hotel.

Shaw's American Plan includes superb meals in the daily rates. The dining room is also open to the public by reservation. Fresh Atlantic lobster, salmon, scallops, prime rib and Island lamb are but a few of the offerings on their extensive menu.

Season: June through September
Major credit cards
Innkeepers: Robbie and Pam Shaw
Brackley Beach, PEI
C1E 1Z3
(902) 672-2022

Shaw's Hotel

Strathgartney Country Inn

STRATHGARTNEY COUNTRY INN

Built in 1863 by Robert Bruce Stewart of Scotland, Strathgartney once occupied some 67,000 acres of land on Prince Edward Island's south shore. Next to Samuel Cunard, the Stewarts were the largest landowners on the island.

Gerald and Martha Gabriel purchased the homestead and 30 acres of the picturesque countryside in 1986. Workshops in painting, writing, photography, pottery and weaving are some of the events offered at Strathgartney throughout the summer. The inn contains 10 guest rooms.

Season: inn, May through September; dining room, late June to early September

Major Credit Cards
Innkeepers: Gerald and Martha Gabriel
R R #3
Bonshaw, PEI
C0A 1C0
(902) 675-4711

THE WEST POINT LIGHTHOUSE

Erected in 1875 and manned until 1963, the Island's tallest lighthouse now offers 10 guest rooms, including a bridal suite, as well as a licensed dining room, patio and gift shop.

This automated lighthouse is still in operation and stands at the southwestern tip of Prince Edward Island, facing the warm waters of the Northumberland Strait. Guests can wander the dunes, swim, build sandcastles and enjoy the romance of this one-of-a-kind location. The dining room is open to guests and the general public and specializes in local fare, such as clam chowder and chunky lobster stew.

Season: mid-May through September
Visa and MasterCard
Innkeeper: Carol Livingstone
R R #2
O'Leary, PEI
C0B 1V0
(902) 859-3605

INDEX